"Many people make documentary movies; Dorothy Fadiman crafts crusades. She's a force of nature, relentless in her pursuit of accuracy and excellence, unremittingly progressive, and yet canny and strategic in the way she develops her arguments. Reading about how she does this is equal to a Master's Degree in Communications."

— Peter Coyote, Actor/Author/Emmy Award–winning narrator of more than 100 documentary productions

"Combining the political passion of the '60s and '70s with a DIY approach now familiar on YouTube, Fadiman embodies the best of both generations, a fusion that makes this book indispensable to all those interested in documenting their own era or engaging with their own times."

— Marsha Kinder is Professor of Critical Studies and Founding Director of The Labyrinth Project at USC's School of Cinematic Arts.

"This insightful work is 'the handbook' for any filmmaker who is thinking about producing a personal documentary. Fadiman's films have made a difference and this book will show you, step by step, how your work can too. *Producing with Passion* is a must read for anyone setting out to make social change media."

— Mitchell Block's distribution company, Direct Cinema Limited, has handled many documentaries and shorts including more than 60 Oscar nominees and winners.

"In the television industry, we are deluged with scripts and ideas for programs. What stands out are the few original voices. This book brings together inspiring guidance with practical suggestions for how to discover and develop your own vision so that, as your project evolves, the work remains truly original."

— Jeremiah Bosgang is the Executive Vice President, Television for SONY BMG Music Entertainment. He has held executive posts at NBC, Fox, MTV and the Howard Stern Production Company, and has written for *Saturday Night Live, In Living Color* and *The Best Damn Sports Show Period.*

"*Producing with Passion* is a must-have resource for those interested in producing or making documentaries. Whether you have a big budget or a very limited one, this book will guide you through the process of bringing your vision to life."

— Kari Ann Morgan, *Microfilmmaker Magazine*

"As the world gets smaller, it's the smaller films that make the biggest impact. Fadiman and Levelle have crafted an excellent guide that provides step by step support for the novice documentary filmmaker. It's about time somebody championed films that make money AND make a difference!"

— Catherine Clinch, Publisher *www.MomsDigitalWorld.com*

"One of the best ways to learn the craft of filmmaking is to apprentice with an artisan. Dorothy Fadiman is not only a master at the art of making films, she is a great teacher who is willing to share her experience with us in her new book, *Producing with Passion.*"

— Stewart Cheifet, Executive Producer, Producer, Director & Writer of over one thousand programs for PBS including *Computer Chronicles, A Life of Dancing, Return of Apollo 11*

PRODUCING WITH PASSION

Dorothy Fadiman
&
Tony Levelle

MICHAEL WIESE PRODUCTIONS

Published by Michael Wiese Productions
3940 Laurel Canyon Blvd. – Suite 1111
Studio City, CA 91604
(818) 379-8799, (818) 986-3408 (FAX).
mw@mwp.com
www.mwp.com

Cover design by MWP
Interior design by William Morosi
Copyedited by Paul Norlen
Printed by McNaughton & Gunn

Manufactured in the United States of America

Library of Congress Cataloging-in-Publication Data
Fadiman, Dorothy.
  Producing with passion / Dorothy Fadiman and Tony Levelle.
     p. cm.
  Includes bibliographical references and index.
  ISBN 978-1-932907-44-5
  1. Motion pictures--Production and direction. I. Levelle, Tony, 1944- II. Title.
  PN1995.9.P7F33 2008
  791.4302'32–dc22
                                        2008009425

Mixed Sources
Product group from well-managed
forests and other controlled sources
www.fsc.org Cert no. SW-COC-002283
© 1996 Forest Stewardship Council

FSC

TABLE OF CONTENTS

ACKNOWLEDGMENTS

This book is the outgrowth of thirty years of filmmaking. I am deeply grateful to hundreds of people for their commitment to working with me to produce twenty documentary films. The full list of those who've given hands-on help, financial contributions, and advice would fill a dozen pages.

This list is only partial. Almost all of these are people worked directly on more than one film.

Videography and editing: Amy Hill, Blake McHugh, Bob Moore, Bridget Louis, Clemencia Macias, Cotton Coulson, David Espar, Daniel Meyers, Henock Hailu, John V. Fante, Kristin Atwell, Katie Larkin, Lise Braden, Matthew Luotto, Michael Carrier , Mika Ferris, Nila Bogue, Peter Carnochan, Rick Keller, Robert Pacelli, Roopa Parameswaran, and Shenaz Zack.

Music and sound: Alex de Grassi, Dave Nelson, Erika Luckett, Jan Lovett Keen, Stephen Hill, and Stephen Longstreth.

Images: Barry Brukoff, Dean Cutler, Jeanette Stobie, Ken Jenkins, Peter Girard, Sisse Brimberg, Stephen P. Mangold, and Wernher Krutein.

Production and outreach collaboration: Anilise Hyllmon, Beth Seltzer, Bruce O'Dell, Danielle Renfrew, Gayle Whitaker, Kat LaEstrange, Kathy Kneer, Katie Peterson, Laura Wigod, Matthew Segal, Melissa Wener, Molly Tanenbaum, Rob Cohen, and Tashana Landray.

Additional support, from personal guidance to pro bono volunteering to funding assistance: Dr. Agonafer Tekalegne, Carla Henry, Danny McGuire, David Andrews, Davidi Gilo, Diana Bebbington, Don Lauro, Dorothy Lyddon, Ekta Bansal, Eve Eisenberg, Foster Gamble, Freddie Long, Gopi

Gopalkrishnan, Jim Fadiman, Jim Moses, Jo Killen, Joan Armer, Jonathan Simon, Karen F. Grove, Maribea Berry, Mary Anne Raywid, Mitchell Block, Nesru Oumer, Oz Crosby, Peggy Kenny, Phyllis Cole, Rita Thrasher, Robert Levenson, Sarah Jane Holcombe, Shamaya Gilo, Sharon Bergeron, Susan Thompson, Terry Beresford, Theron Horton, Tom Layton, Victoria Nichols, and to the hundreds of people who allowed me to interview them.

A special thanks to the people who read the manuscript-in-progress: David L. Brown, who offered many suggestions that improved the manuscript greatly; and to Jane Kinzler, Jennifer Myronuk, Kacy McClure, and Kristen Schulz Oliver.

Thanks also to Patsy O'Sullivan and the people of Bonane, County Kerry, Ireland for giving a warm Irish welcome and opening their homes to our crew when we shot a documentary to test the advice and how-to instructions in this book.

And with deep appreciation, I thank Michael Wiese, who said to me thirty years ago, when I was struggling to write a book about light, "Did you ever think of making a film?" His question gave birth to my first film, *Radiance*.

Introduction

How Can a Film Make a Difference?

1. *A film that reflects your true passion can have an impact for generations. This book gives you the tools to envision, produce, and finish such a film.*
2. *As a documentary filmmaker, you have the means to open people's eyes and bring them into another world.*
3. *One of the major challenges in making your film will be keeping your focus from beginning to end.*
4. *This book is divided into three parts:*
   a. *Getting clear about your vision*
   b. *Sustaining your intention as you produce the film*
   c. *Launching your finished movie*

A film that reflects your true passion will carry with it a special energy, a vital sense of purpose that can have an impact for generations.

Today, after working on the script of my latest film *Stealing America*, one of my interns sat with me and we reviewed the master DVD for the re-release of my "oldest" film, *Radiance*, which was made three decades ago.

This fall, we are going to be offering *Radiance* in packages of a dozen for people to give as Christmas gifts. We already have orders for the package.

I didn't think of making something that would last generations when I made *Radiance*. Instead, I only tried to do one thing — to tell what was true for me.

This book tells you how to make a film about what is true for you.

We will show you how to harness your inspiration, make a documentary, and finish it, with your vision intact.

Each chapter takes you on a journey along well-traveled film-making highways, as well as little-known byways. All these roads lead to resources that will help you stay true to your vision as you face the inevitable challenges of filmmaking. Why is this so important? With every hard-won step forward, you realize more fully, every day, that it is *your* vision that will breathe life into your completed work.

When you make a documentary, you hold the potential to open people's eyes and take them beyond their usual way of seeing the world. A filmmaker possesses the means to draw viewers in as a story unfolds and introduce them to other real-ities. Whether you are documenting nature, human nature, or the latest technology, the audience enters another realm through your film.

Several years ago, I produced *Woman by Woman*, a film about village couples living in rural India, who provide social ser-vices to their communities. As my cinematographer and I drove down dusty back roads, passing ox-drawn carts and one-room mud huts, I was struck by the challenge of reaching audiences in the West with a story set in this "other world" separated from modern life in so many ways. Throughout our time in India, I stayed alert, determined to find moments that would bridge these worlds.

While filming an interview with a newlywed husband, the answer appeared. He spoke about not being allowed to meet or even see his bride until their wedding day. He confided to us during the interview how nervous he was about finally seeing the woman he was to be with for the rest of his life.

During the editing, we crafted the scene so that the audience could enter his demanding day to day world, in which there is no electricity or running water. At the same time, we wanted viewers to empathize with his human feelings, which are universal. When the film is screened, we first see him cut his crops with a scythe, and carry them to his shed on his head.

Then, he sits down and explains his arranged marriage. It's clear, at first, that Western audiences feel uneasy with his tradition, of not looking at his bride until they are married. (When viewers shift in their seats, it is a sure sign of unrest.) Not seeing the person you will marry is so different from the Western ideal of falling in love. Then, when he goes on to describe lifting his bride's veil, he breaks into a huge smile. It's clear that he likes what he sees, very much! When people see his delight, they sigh, chuckle and relax, as they share in his feelings of relief.

As the filmmaker, you have the tools to bring people into another world, in this case a rural scene which has remained virtually unchanged for centuries. At the same time, you can invite them into the present with a universal human experience, like Pawan's smile. The decisions you make about how to choose, and then juxtapose, the elements in your film are what will make the final piece yours.

As a filmmaker, you have the means to tell stories from the smallest details of life, to situations beyond comprehension. More than ever before, there are opportunities, through a range of new distribution outlets, for filmmakers to make documentaries that open people's minds and hearts and that will be seen by many. Whatever ignites your passion has the potential to touch others. Whatever subject you choose, there are now ways to reach individuals and organizations around the world who can see and use your documentary.

KEEPING YOUR FOCUS

When you make a film, one of the major challenges is maintaining your focus until completion. At every step along the way, unplanned problems — technical challenges, financial worries, interpersonal friction — might throw you off course. Given these inevitable distractions, we want to help you find ways to maintain the optimism you had at the beginning. Each chapter of this book has suggestions to help you stay connected to your intention. No matter how exhausted you are, or how difficult a scene may be to edit together, no matter how unresolved an interaction with a crew member may seem, the stories and suggestions in this book have been written with these goals in mind: to help you solve problems, and remind you of ways to rekindle your spark.

I've spent thirty years searching out practical approaches to get my productions funded, finished, and seen. In this book, I share what I've learned, and suggest ideas for how you can adapt my "solutions" so they work for you.

USING THIS BOOK

This book is like a traveler's guide. As you set out to make a film, the information and commentaries will help you decide which direction to take. We recommend ways to get there and suggest options to consider once you've arrived, but the journey is yours.

The first few chapters will help you get clear about your overall vision, and give you tips about pulling together your resources. There are many books on filmmaking which focus on shooting and editing. This book does not. The first half of the book is about charting your course, and preparing to succeed in making it all the way to the summit and back. We do not discuss "shooting" until halfway through the book. Why? Because to us, the essence of your film will be what you bring to it. We provide encouragement and propose guidelines for maintaining your vision as you shoot, edit, and produce the movie. The final chapters put together useful suggestions for launching your project into the world.

This book gives you information, suggestions, and assumes that — putting those together — you will find your way, yourself, to your destination.

Films have the power to reach countless people. When you make a film, you have the means to make a difference.

Let's start.

CHAPTER 1

Trusting Your Instincts

1. Passion is a special energy.

2. The momentum of that energy keeps you going.

3. Trust your intuition.

4. How do you deal with distractions and doubts?

5. Prepare for what it takes to finish a project.

Passion and Intuition, the Magical Connection That Will Keep You Going

Producing your own movie takes passion. You can make a film for hire without it, but to envision and complete your own film will take a special energy, which I call "passion." When you find a subject that inspires you and truly captures your attention, you tap into a wellspring of vitality that gives you the stamina you'll need to face the challenges of making a movie.

Once you begin, you soon learn that the demands of film-making are continuous. Every day presents opportunities to be creative, to learn something new — and to fail. I've learned repeatedly that there are no easy answers. After trying for years to "get it right," I finally discovered the wisdom of listening to my inner sense of "knowing what to do." Following my passion has led me to trust my intuition. That sense of being on-purpose gives me the direction I need.

Sometimes filmmakers find it necessary to work on subjects outside of their interests, usually because they need to make money, sometimes to help a friend. At other times, people choose a topic because it is popular or perhaps someone else urged them to pursue an idea that isn't coming from the filmmaker at all. These films, which aren't connected to the

1

producer's own vision, rarely have the same momentum as projects that are truly yours.

However, even when you are the source of the idea, making a film that is truly yours is still difficult. If you don't have enough support, financial or collegial or from your own belief in yourself, it's hard to keep that flame burning. So when you make a commitment to the idea for your own film, make a decision that you will consciously stay close to what is true for you as you go forward.

MY STORY

While harnessing the spark for my own first film, I learned the importance of listening to, and trusting, my intuition. The seed was planted when I was on retreat. I had settled into the final week of a month-long time out from my daily routine. I was in the tropics. I remember the sounds — a cascade of raindrops pelting on leaves outside the screened openings of my cottage. I had just read a passage on spiritual awakening, and was beginning to meditate, listening to the storm.

As my mind cleared, I became aware of another sound, apart from the rain. A voice seemed to be coming from somewhere inside of me, asking this question: "May I fill you with light?" Inhaling deeply, I breathed out a silent "Yes," and a shimmering radiance began to pour into my body. I felt as if I was floating in a sea of light. I trembled, not in fear, but in surrender. I knew, without knowing, that the brilliance flooding me was what saints and mystics describe, an infusion of a force that lifts them into another reality.

I have no idea how long the experience lasted. As the light began to fade, a sense of purpose filled me. I returned home from the retreat, and began reading everything I could find, from scientific research to the memoirs of saints. I was compelled to create some vehicle that would communicate the power of this light. I had no idea where to begin.

At first, I decided to imitate my husband, and write a book. He wrote non-fiction books, and I tried to follow his lead and do what he'd done. It wasn't a natural choice for me to try to spell out in words something so experiential. I ignored my doubts, persevered, and went through years of frustration, working on a book about light. But words on paper couldn't capture the essence of what I felt. I still have file boxes filled with my earnest efforts. I was discouraged, and nearly quit trying, but didn't give up.

One day, ten years after the initial experience, a filmmaker showed up in my life… literally on my doorstep. He lived in another city, and was in my neighborhood. He had heard about my futile efforts and was attracted to the project. Right then and there he challenged me. He said, "I heard you were trying to write a book about light. Did you ever think of making a movie?" When he asked that question, I knew, intuitively, that the answer was "Yes." I could feel in my bones that film-making was the right medium for this project, and for me.

IGNITING THE SPARK

I knew nothing about producing movies, but that didn't stop me. The filmmaker offered to work with me, and our collaboration led to my first film, *Radiance: The Experience of Light.*

He was the Producer and I was the Director. At that point, I didn't even know one from the other, but I knew we had to make that movie.

Although passion kept me going for ten years before that meeting, the actual making of the movie required that I learn a synthesis of passion, intuition, and a keen sense of "inner knowing." This synthesis has stayed with me ever since.

Radiance wasn't the book my husband would have written, or the film that the filmmaker would have made without me. It was mine. And, as we worked together, I realized that I needed help to bring it into being. Like most independent filmmakers who take this journey, the inspiration was mine, but it took a team effort to manifest it.

Radiance grew from my passion born from my own experience of "light." While I was making the film, I felt compelled to convey that spirit. Which is, I believe, why *Radiance* continues to be in demand today, two generations later.

Last year, I quietly put *Radiance* up on the Internet Archive (*www.archive.com*). We have never promoted its presence there, at all. So far, without any advertising, it has had over ten thousand viewings and is approaching three thousand downloads. (I take a glimpse every week or two, and the numbers just keep steadily going up.)

Through all the teaching I've done over the years, I know for a fact that everyone has an innate sense of "knowing when you know." Filmmaking requires that you learn to trust that sense of knowing, and then recognize what is going to work for you. From that first film onward, the fire of passion has lit the path, with intuition by my side as my guide.

Choosing a Subject

Producer/director Jacques Perrin's lifelong interest in the natural world is evident in his film, *Winged Migration* (2001). The movie is a loving portrayal of different species of birds as they complete their yearly migration. The stunning photography and story brings the mystery and beauty of the planet's birds alive for the viewer. After seeing *Winged Migration*, people look at birds through new eyes.

Perrin may have been inspired to make this film about birds when he saw another filmmaker's documentary about Canadian geese. The film he made became "his" when he committed to his vision to create a work that shows, through his eyes, the freedom and beauty of birds in flight.

Choosing a Subject That Has Life

We all have passions. Sometimes they're hard to identify and even harder to harness, because they may be abstract or unruly or silent or even invisible. Recognizing an idea that will ring true for you means dipping into the passions that run through you like deep rivers. They flow with mysterious, life-giving water. Those driving impulses, the ones that will get you to the finish line, register for different people in different ways. For me, the signal is physical — especially when I am looking toward making a film, I get "trills of truth." When an idea or an event moves me deeply, I get goose bumps. The hairs on my arms stand up, as if they are listening. When I feel this sensation, I stop whatever I am doing and ask myself, "Okay… What just happened?"

Your own alert to pay attention may or may not be physical. Some people breathe faster, some more deeply. Some feel giddy, some deeply calm; others simply feel energized, as if a force is moving through them. Whatever your signal, when you feel drawn toward a subject, you will have a sense that something is calling you, maybe whispering in your ear, maybe screaming out your name. Some people say literally, "It had my name on it." The catalyst that triggers the response, beckoning you to create something new, can be ignited by a person, a headline, a poem, a dream, a fragrance — there is no one way.

What these "callings" have in common is that you feel compelled to make something happen.

Imagining Possibilities

If nothing comes to mind to ignite a spark for you, use your imagination. Imagine possibilities. As you fall asleep, fantasize movies you could make. When you are standing in line in the supermarket or stalled in traffic, brainstorm scenes. Reading the newspaper or a magazine, watching someone else's documentary or a TV show or the news or even a soap opera can generate ideas. Does something "click"?

As you explore possibilities, several subjects may vie for attention. Some people stop there, because they can't decide! If you want to make a film, but the "right idea" is not obvious, or you are having difficulty choosing one to develop, take time out. You might gather with some friends and brainstorm. You could set aside an hour or two to walk in nature or sit in meditation and see what bubbles up.

Just "opening the floor" and asking for ideas, will start a process. Fresh ideas will come to mind, until you recognize one that is yours to pursue.

QUESTIONS THAT MIGHT HELP
YOU CHOOSE A SUBJECT

When I give workshops, these are some of the questions I throw out to help people find ideas for their films.

- What are some of the most dramatic moments you have you lived through?
- Who are some of the most memorable people you have known?
- Where do you find the greatest beauty?
- What subjects fascinate you?
- What frightens you?
- What angers you?
- What worries you?
- What do you love to do?

Films that will be of genuine interest to someone else are almost always based on ideas that come from your own knowledge, experiences, concerns, and yearnings. The word "authenticity" may be overused. However, there are times when authenticity best describes why someone tunes in to a film. When a film-maker conveys an authentic experience, people pick that up. There's a tendency to diminish the importance of your own experience, through modesty or shyness or lack of confidence. Making a film calls for you to believe in yourself.

Don't get caught looking only for big ideas. Intimate ideas are often the most universal. Some of the most engaging films are simply an up-close look at a single subject.

For years I had been taking broken household appliances to a tiny store near my home. I loved the way the patient repairmen kept toasters and blenders out of the landfill by bringing them back to life with their tools and attention. That dedication inspired *Fix-It Shops: An Endangered Species,* a five-minute film documenting this ecological microcosm just around the corner from where I live.

As you scan the horizon, don't forget to look close to home.

FRIENDS, COLLEAGUES AND COMPANIONS

As a rule of thumb, it seems to take about a year to make a thirty-minute documentary, on average. (Some projects take a few months, and some take ten years.) How will you sustain your excitement about an idea for a year or more?

One way to stay energized is to be in touch with people who reflect your passion and energy back to you. Filmmakers find these companions in a variety of ways. Often, they are friends and family members. In recent years, filmmakers sometimes find these people through Internet user groups. Some may develop through e-mail exchanges with people who start out as strangers, but who are interested in the same subject about which you are passionate. These virtual connections might become close colleagues. During a production, I try to stay in touch with people who share my vision and interest.

If you want to have a "normal" social life while you make a movie, you have to make it happen. I find that if I don't make a conscious effort to keep up a social life, I begin to limit inter-actions to the people on the film team. Sometimes I go for months without seeing a movie or visiting friends — except those who are connected to production. You certainly don't have to be this strict, but the fact is the more focused you are, the more likely you are to complete your project. One special bonus is that this kind of focused intensity leads to intimate relationships with your home team. Because of their intensity, some of these relationships last a lifetime.

I have learned to accept the fact that not everyone in my life will come along for the ride. Some people don't appreciate who I become when I am in the middle of making a movie. I have parted ways with friends who find this style of friend-ship — my not being available when "in production" — too unsatisfying. With others, who are more patient, our friend-ship deepens because they accept who I am, and appreciate what I am doing. They understand that my connection is still there with them, but my time and energy are pouring into the film.

DISTRACTIONS AND DOUBT

Creative energy is precious, but your connection to it can, at times, be fragile. At certain points in every project, your energy will diminish or even disappear. This dip in interest is natural, and happens to everyone. At times, the sense of losing touch with the project may be overwhelming, and you just want to quit. The omnipresent danger at any point along the way is succumbing to doubt, and slipping into a downward spiral in which hope seems beyond reach.

One of the reasons filmmakers lose heart is that other people discourage them along the way. While you develop your idea, you've got to maintain your focus. Some people will love your idea, but others may criticize you. Certain comments will instill doubt. You might hear, "No one wants to talk openly about that" or, "That's already been done." Some people just need to play devil's advocate, because it is their way of being involved, and it's not about you or your subject. You do need to consider the source.

Recently, one of my relatives heard I was making a film about the presidential election of 2004. She said, "You have so much talent. Why waste your time on this? The election's over!" I listened, and almost began to defend myself. Then I realized that she was not politically active, and really didn't understand where I was going with this project. I thanked her for her candid feedback, and went on to show a work-in-progress of that film to sold-out screenings across the country. When someone tries to discourage me, I consider the input, and then sort through what they've said. If, after doing that, the project still feels right, my resolve deepens.

Unasked-for Attention

When you make a film, the more passionate and committed you become, the more others will be attracted to the project. Some may want to work with you; others care about the subject and want to see the film finished, and in distribution. Along with the magnetic pull that magnetizes others to you, you may find that there is a shadow side, not only at the beginning, but along the way as well. As you progress, in addition to being the creator, you must also become a gatekeeper.

Often people who are attracted to the project may offer their services, even when you don't want help. Be selective. Others may try to influence your project because they identify with it, and feel they can add needed input. Some recognize the power in what you are doing and want to be part of that for their own reasons. You may or may not want any of these people working with you, even as volunteers. Be not only selective, but also protective.

At first, you may be flattered, but be careful. If people want your time, or try to press their opinions on you, the basic rule is to listen, learn what you can, and thank them for their input. Always return to checking in with your own inner sense of what's right for you. Remember always, it is *your* project. If you don't know whether or not to trust someone who comes to you, someone you don't know, do background research. At every stage, and at every level of the project, the archetype "Darth Vader" — a threat to the vision — may show up. This disturbance in the force may be external, or it may come from your own fears.

Your Own Doubts

One obstacle that you might face is doubt about your own abilities. You may find yourself thinking, "I have always dreamed about doing this, but I don't know if I can really pull it together." If the prospect of making a film frightens you, but you still feel drawn, I say "go for it" — even though I can promise you that it will probably be more challenging, time consuming, and character building than you expect.

If you have doubt about not having the right facts to proceed, or not enough information, the first step is to find out what you need to know. (If you need to do more research, fact checking is an excellent task for volunteers.) When you do more research, and fill in the blanks, you can answer these doubts and press forward.

Remember, as your project moves beyond where you started, and as you get new insights and information, to let the production evolve. The core idea will have a voice of its own, and this voice will tell you which direction to go.

The new direction might involve filming different interviewees, shooting more B-roll footage for cover or doing more research or adding certain stills. The new direction may even mean releasing someone who has been on the team for a while, and bringing on someone new. Be open to change, and stay flexible.

GETTING STUCK

Input about what to do next, as you proceed, will come from many sources — what you see as you watch your footage and your edited cuts, what you read, input from others, and from your own intuition. Make plenty of notes as you go. Keep notebooks and/or files of all this new information.

To take full advantage of the ideas and opinions of others, you need to be willing — at different times — to hold the reins and take over, while sometimes you will need to let them go and let yourself be guided. Stay open to this back and forth, as you learn to recognize when you need help and how to use it well.

Being willing to change direction when you get new information is not a sign of weakness. Be ready to accept input, if it improves the work, and protect your idea if you sense that feedback will weaken it.

When you find an idea that "has your name on it," these challenges along the way give you a chance to do reality checks and learn what you need to know to carry out the vision.

RESTORING YOUR ENERGY

If you begin to lose your "juice," there are ways to get refreshed. Some of these are so obvious they may seem cliché, and get overlooked.

For most people the best thing to do is to take a break, at least a couple of days off. On those days, sleep until you wake up naturally (no alarm clocks) and take naps.

Give yourself "a real break." If you've been indoors too long, just going outside more often will refresh you. If you enjoy hiking, biking, gardening, or anything physical, those activities help restore a balance.

Give yourself time to do these things. When you feel physically rejuvenated, it is much easier to tap back into your goal and remember where you are headed.

FINISHING THE PROJECT

Finishing an independent film is one of the most difficult parts of filmmaking. Only an idea that captures your attention will be strong enough to carry you through to the end. Without a strong connection to your subject, it's almost impossible to sustain the drive to complete a film. The will to carry on to the end will be generated from merging your intention, your willingness to learn and reflect on what you are learning, and your own passionate sense of purpose.

At every point along the way, a balance of passion and reflection comes into play. How to turn that mix into action is between the lines on every page of this book.

You may be the only person in the world who can tell a certain story in a particular way. Remember this: An idea that brings you to life means that the way you make that film will be unique.

KEY POINTS

- You need passion to make (and finish) your own movie.

- When you choose a subject with life for you, you tap into a wellspring of energy.

- Filmmaking requires that you trust your intuition.

- Films that emerge from your own knowledge, experiences, hopes, and concerns will be of interest to others.

- The strength of the core idea, and your commitment to it, will carry you through the challenges it takes to make a film.

- As you go forward, your energy may diminish. This dip in interest is natural and happens to everyone.

- Learn to differentiate between input that makes a contribution, and input that becomes a distraction.

- The core idea, and the elements related to it, are continually changing and evolving.

CHAPTER 2

FOCUSING YOUR ENERGIES

1. *Set limits on your project from the beginning.*
2. *Let the project inform you about which way it wants to go.*
3. *Look for, and find, the key idea in your project.*
4. *Ask yourself, "What do I want to accomplish?"*
5. *If you don't frame your idea, the project may become unmanageable.*
6. *Create a one-sheet description to define the project.*

If you don't set limits on your project from the beginning, you may never finish! One of the main challenges filmmakers face is going overboard: doing too much research, shooting too many interviews, coming up with too many ideas, spending too much money, and taking too long to edit the film.

To finish a film, you have to decide how best to use what you have to work with. You cannot predict that your resources will grow. You may or may not raise more money as you go. You may attract more volunteers, but you can't count on it.

So, be realistic. Don't expect miracles, and put together what you can — without going into debt, cutting yourself off from friends and family, or getting sick.

I've learned all this the hard way.

The magic words are focus, focus, and focus. If you can focus, you can pace yourself. And if you can pace yourself, you will have time for a relatively normal life as well.

Ideally, a good film can be described in one strong sentence. Writing that sentence will help you focus. The sentence should include:

1. Subject;

2. Verb (action);

3. Purpose.

Funders, for example, expect you to be able to say what you are doing and why, succinctly. For example:

1. Radiance (subject);

2. brings together the light in nature with spiritual illumination (what the film does);

3. to create a tapestry which connects the day-to-day world with the infinite (why).

This chapter is about focusing your energies and setting limits, so you can finish — and finish without exhausting yourself and your resources.

How to Increase Your Chances of Finishing Your Film

- At the beginning of the film, focus on the subject and set limits. Without a focus and a goal, you can end up shooting, raising money, interviewing people, and tweaking scenes forever.

- Set your aim: Decide what you hope to accomplish with this film.

- Decide on the scope of the film — and be realistic about length and budget. Is the film you envision feasible and practical? Make it doable.

- Ask people (or do research) and find out, has it already been done? If so, what about your film will be unique?

- Do you have, or can you gain, access to the people and material you think you will need? If you need to do that, find out how you can!

- Figure out what kinds of research you would need to do.

FINDING A BALANCE

You will need to start someplace — with an idea and a plan — and then allow your vision to evolve as you work. Keep your goals in mind, and as you learn more, meet new people, and start shooting, your focus will develop and may change. You cannot predict at the outset how your project might take off later.

For example, you might decide on a main character at the beginning of your interviewing, and not know who the main character really is until well into the project! We assumed Molly Hale, a woman who had suffered a spinal cord injury, would be the "lead" in *Moment by Moment*. Halfway through, we realized that her husband Jeramy, who had been by her side through her years of struggle and triumph, was at least as important. The main character turned out to be two people, Jeramy and Molly!

Identifying Your Premise

Once you settle on a subject, it is necessary to frame your idea as a way of defining the scope and setting limits at the start. *Any independent filmmaker can tell you that a film project has the potential to absorb all of your money, all of your time, and all of your energy.* As the production proceeds, related ideas will tempt you to expand your focus; your goal should be to protect and nurture the heart of the story that you want to tell.

In *Moment by Moment,* when I chose to expand my core characters to include Jeramy, Molly's husband, I still remained true to my original idea, which was to follow Molly's healing journey.

One way to frame your idea is to define your goal. Ask yourself, "What do I want to accomplish?" The answer to that question will reveal what is most important to you, personally, about your movie.

By keeping in mind what you want to accomplish, you can be alert when seductive side issues begin to pull you away from your purpose.

ONE FILMMAKER'S SUCCESS AT FINDING AND FOLLOWING A SINGLE PREMISE

Michael Moore is well known for focusing his documentaries on a single premise. *Roger & Me* is apparently built on one question: "What if I set out to ask GM's CEO, Roger B. Smith, how he feels about the damage done to Flint, Michigan, when General Motors closed the plant and threw thirty thousand people out of work?"

Microphone in hand and camera crew in tow, Moore set out to interview Smith. In his pursuit of an interview, Moore managed to talk to GM guards, GM employees, and the unemployed people of Flint. He toured a new jail, and filmed a high-society lawn party. The comedic premise of a rumpled, unemployed troublemaker trying to put the CEO of GM on the spot hooked the audience. Along the way, Moore achieved his real objective: He showed what happened to Flint and its people after the GM plant closed.

As you go forward, ask yourself: "What is the key idea at the heart of my movie?" The key idea will act as a spine that links the other elements: interviews, on-location scenes, factual information, graphics, and special effects.

What Do You Want to Accomplish?

When you clarify what you want to achieve, you will begin to feel that the production is finally rolling forward.

There is a natural momentum built into every project. Once your project is "in motion," commit to doing something on the film every day. Even if you just scribble down some notes, you'll soon feel a magnetic pull, matching your own effort.

Here is a breakdown of the journey of one of my films *When Abortion Was Illegal: Untold Stories.*

a. The single premise

With the film *When Abortion Was Illegal: Untold Stories,* I focused on a single premise: That the people who lived through the days of back-alley abortions, by telling their personal stories, could educate a generation with no memory of that era.

b. My goals

One of my goals was to reach a generation of young adults who had grown up after *Roe v. Wade,* without a frame of reference for what it was like to live at a time when abortion was illegal and women were dying in back alleys.

c. The momentum

The project attracted women who had gone through illegal abortions, who had never told their stories before, as well as the doctors, nurses, and others who risked being arrested to provide safe care. As the generation that lived through these experiences aged, their stories were on the verge of being lost.

d. The response

By staying with one theme — dramatic stories of the era — I invited viewers to empathize with the human experiences of those who had lived through the suffering and danger.

Now, more than fifteen years after its release, we still get a steady stream of requests for that film. Within the last few years we have sold forty thousand copies of a DVD which includes excerpts from it.

Any topic is potentially inexhaustible. I could have spent years on different aspects of that issue. However, I chose a single topic: people telling their untold stories.

e. A note: You don't need to "do it all" with one film

A film with a strong point will trigger curiosity. You don't need to talk about all aspects of a subject in your film. People are eager, if interested, to put the rest of the puzzle together in other ways.

What I did, in addition to *When Abortion Was Illegal*, was make two additional films, with each taking on a different focus. From *Danger to Dignity* profiles underground networks, and the struggle to make abortion legal. *The Fragile Promise of Choice* looks at the current situation ranging from clinic violence to regressive legislation.

The issues and dramas that surround abortion are multiple. Every one is worthy of documentation, and they all engaged me.

But I had to circumscribe one to start.

Setting Goals

Too often filmmakers end up with boxes of unfinished elements because they attempted to do too much. After deciding to focus on those untold stories in When Abortion Was Illegal,

I asked myself, "What would I need to make and to complete this one film?" I came up with a list:

Interviewees

1. Women who had had illegal abortions, who would be telling their stories for the first time outside their immediate family.

2. Professionals (doctors, nurses, clergy, lawyers) who defied abortion laws as acts of conscience.

3. How many? Based on past experience, I hoped to find about ten interviewees for the final film.

Time

Given the urgency (in 1991 there was the danger of the Supreme Court overturning *Roe v. Wade*), I planned to finish in less than a year.

Money

To interview people from different parts of the United States, I needed to add travel costs into the budget (in addition to a videographer, an editor, appropriate music, and other basic costs).

Aiming for national television and PBS meant that I needed high production values. The camera work, images, and audio had to be broadcast quality.

Distribution

My goal was to get the film out to as many people as possible, so I aimed for national television, PBS, educational markets, and private screenings — all of which happened.

(What I didn't know then, and wouldn't have put on the list as a goal, is that *When Abortion Was Illegal* would be nominated for an Oscar and would win the Corporation for Public Broadcasting Gold Medal!)

With my thumbnail sketch of project requirements, I was able to assess what I might need to complete the film. The list enabled me to get started without feeling overwhelmed. As I worked on the film, my needs changed, but I had a place from which to start.

Framing the Idea

The potential for doing background research, searching for interviewees, and tweaking a script is unlimited! If, for example, you have too much information, or too many interviewees, your goal begins to get fragmented. Some filmmakers never finish because they never feel they've done enough.

How do you know when to stop gathering material, doing interviews, or researching?

You have to ask yourself, "What do I actually need?"

Taking stock is necessary at every stage of your film, including the stage when you are shooting footage. (See Chapter 12 for a description of field production.) When we were shooting location footage for *Woman by Woman*, we became enchanted with colorful, dramatic, poignant images of India. We shot tape after tape of street scenes and villages. We could have made do with half of what we gathered. But we were drawn deeper and deeper into the mysterious beauty of India. We finally did run out of money, and then stopped. If I had been more judicious — or spent more time on preproduction — I would have stopped much sooner and still had more than enough footage. Logging the footage took months! (See Chapter 15 for a description of logging.)

Limiting your idea to a focused premise gives you a yardstick. Ask yourself, as well as you can early on, does this B-roll footage, this interview, or this research, support the point of the film?

THE PROJECT DESCRIPTION

Early in the process of making your film, you may find it useful to create a "one-sheet" for your film.

A one-sheet is exactly what the name implies: one sheet of paper, on which information is provided about the filmmaker and the film.

The one-sheet typically serves as a way to introduce a particular film or a series of films. It will often contain a variety of information, both images and text, about the film. The name of the filmmaker and the title of the film should appear prominently.

Begin by writing a single sentence that describes your project and then expand on that sentence until you have a concise description of your project that fits on part of one sheet of paper.

This first pass should include full contact information.

As your project evolves, some common elements you might add to the one-sheet would include:

- Biographical information

- Photograph(s) of the filmmaker

- Cover artwork for the release

- Names of other films or awards.

- List of credits

The description will eventually evolve in two directions: one for publicity as a flyer, and one into a detailed treatment, which can be used for everything from press releases, to giving new interns an overview of the project, to an introduction to a funding proposal.

Developing Your Idea

Once you have your subject in mind, and have a sense of where you are going with that idea — even though you might not yet have raised any money or shot any footage — you should take a crack at laying out possible scenarios for your idea, to see how it might look.

Three Ways to Map a Project

☞ Mind map

A mind map is a graphic way to organize information and reveal relationships. One way to make a mind map is to write a key word in the middle of a blank piece of paper, and then to draw branching links to other key words.

☞ Post-Its™ and poster board

Poster boards are very, very useful ways to see, at a glance, the possibilities of a storyboarded progression at the beginning, or the shape of a film partway through. I often use different colored Post-Its to represent different types of information (interviews, narration, archival footage, vérité synch sound scenes, etc.).

☞ Mind dump

When you are really stuck, doing a "mind dump" can break through mental logjams. To do a mind dump, just list everything you can think of on a piece of paper or on the computer screen, then organize it in different ways showing how the pieces might fit together.

MAINTAINING A BALANCE

The eventual success of your film will depend on your ability to find and develop a basic premise that sustains from beginning to end, while allowing for change. Whether you are profiling an individual, documenting a current event, or delving into history, filmmaking requires finding and keeping a balance — somewhere between staying focused and being flexible around the central premise.

Throughout production, ask yourself, "What is this film really about?" Asking that question, letting go of "old pictures," and listening attentively to the answer as it grows, will make the film uniquely "yours."

KEY POINTS

- Starting a film is relatively easy. Identifying the key theme is harder. Finishing may be the hardest part of all.

- When you frame your idea, you pave the way not only for producing but also finishing your film.

- Related ideas and projects may take you off track, and will tempt you to spread your interests, energies, and time. Your goal should be to protect and nurture the heart of the story that you want to tell.

- A film project has the potential to absorb all of your money, all of your time, and all of your life. Your job is to set limits.

- The frame for your film will change and evolve as you work.

- Write a one-sheet project description to frame and define your project.

CHAPTER 3

KNOW YOUR SUBJECT

1. *If you want to make a vibrant film, you must have a genuine understanding of your subject.*

2. *Background research is what you do when you immerse yourself in the material and document what you learn.*

3. *The types of information you will probably use are: books, articles, films, public documents, private documents, and people.*

4. *When you talk to people you might be:*
   - *Gathering information*
   - *Pre-interviewing potential interviewees*

5. *Watch for what I call "The Universal Matching Grant Service."*

To create a vibrant documentary, you need a genuine understanding of your subject. Only then will you be able to use the most relevant facts, find the people who tell the story best, select the ideal images, and locate the places that will give your film depth and dimensionality.

For every subject, there usually already exists a body of information, or at least bits of information, discovered and assembled by people who have studied the topic. Your job is to learn as much as you can about the subject, from their work and on your own. At every step along the way, from fundraising to attracting staff, when people sense that you've done your homework, they will be more open to sharing what they have to offer with you.

BACKGROUND RESEARCH

Background research involves immersing yourself in the subject of your documentary. At some point, you start to see a pattern. When you first begin, explore widely — read books, see films, surf the Internet, maybe visit museums, and, above all, ask for and listen to people's ideas and opinions.

Research will continue throughout production, but at some point you begin to put the pieces together.

When I was doing research for *Why Do These Kids Love School?* I studied different approaches to progressive education. I learned that moving freely (discouraged in strict classroom settings) is an integral element to holistic learning. One scene of the film shows fourth graders stretched out reaching across a table doing math together.

That scene is both "authentic" and, at the same time, visually engaging! I was able to bring together my research (about whole body involvement and collaboration in learning), my purpose (to show this kind of education), and the footage.

When your research gives added relevance to actual footage, that synthesis gives the project vitality. If something "grabs" your interest, follow the lead. Filmmaking is a voyage of discovery — relish the search and be open to the possibilities.

How One Filmmaker's Research Gives His Films Vitality

Ken Burns' films are monuments to the value of background research. His Civil War documentaries are so meticulously researched that historians are said to use them as reference material. Burns does exhaustive research of actual photographs and diaries from the era he is documenting.

Burns has a small research staff that has worked together for years. I think that the quality and quantity of the background research that Burns does contributes greatly to the appeal of his films.

> *The Civil War* (2004), Ken Burns. (A digitally re-mastered set of DVDs was released in 2004.)

You will be surprised where your investigations may lead you. While researching "light" for *Radiance*, I learned about Kirilian photography, which captures images of energy emanating from living objects. With some effort, I tracked down the woman who conducted the original research. In response to my inquiry, she sent me a stack of slides that showed bristling electrical energy radiating from humans and plants. She invited me to use them at no cost because she wanted them seen and used.

KINDS OF INFORMATION

With the Internet and low-cost digital media, one of the hurdles to overcome is that there is so much information. Never before have scholars and lay researchers faced this magnitude of resources. Your challenge, then, is to find the nuggets and trusted sources.

Places to which I turn when researching a film, in roughly the order that I use them, are:

- The Internet
- Articles
- Informational interviews
- Public and private documents
- Books and films

I used to spend weeks on end at the library, making requests on little slips of paper. The librarians used them to find and bring out books, articles, newspapers, and microfiche. Now I do most of the initial research on the Internet.

FINDING PEOPLE AS SOURCES

Once I have done basic Internet research, I come up with a list of names of people I want to try to reach. I say "try" because some of them are essentially "unreachable." But I try.

How do I find these people?

Once I've identified the people I want to reach, I go back to the Internet. I search for e-mail addresses, articles they've written, groups they belong to, places they've spoken: anything that might lead to contact information.

Sometimes it is simple, for example, if an individual publishes a newsletter with contact information. Sometimes I have to pick up the phone and start calling people.

I ask, "Do you know so and so?" or "Do you know how to reach so and so?" or "Do you know anyone who knows," etc. Ninety percent of the time, I eventually reach the person, but not always. Finding people can be a laborious process. Be prepared for mostly hits and some misses.

Once I make contact, I either e-mail or call the person, and usually get a response. Sometimes, I need to repeat the contact several times before I get an answer. I introduce myself with as many credentials as I can put together, including my interest in that person and the subject.

If I reach the person, I ask if this is a good time to speak, or shall we make a telephone date, or if they are nearby, a time to meet. For this "informational interview" I am prepared with brief, specific questions. While the person answers these questions, I am also listening (or reading, if an e-mail) to see if this might be an appropriate interviewee for the film.

As with every other step in production, good relationships are at the heart of filmmaking. By involving other people in your searches, working together, tracing leads, and making surprise connections, you and your partners in the search will uncover treasures you never knew existed!

In one case, my relationship with a film librarian led me to some brilliant archival footage.

Twelve years ago, before I really knew about how to use the Internet for research, I immersed myself in various departments of the Library of Congress for weeks while working on *From Danger to Dignity*. I hoped to find facts, names and documents from the sparsely documented era of back-alley abortions. Some of what I discovered, I could now find online, but not all. Certainly not what I am about to share.

One of my regular stops every few days was the office of the film librarian, the person who tracked down the actual footage for films I found in the card catalogs. She had a personal interest in women's rights, and, as my searches intensified, we became friends.

One morning she rose to greet me as I approached her desk. She motioned for me to follow her as she turned toward the screening booths. Without a word, she led me into a dark cubicle set aside for 35mm films.

She had pulled five reels of a 1920s silent feature. As the film ran, I watched in stunned silence. I had been looking for *anything* from that era that even touched on abortion when even the word was taboo. This precious silent film, the only print in existence, told the poignant story of a "damsel in distress" who had gone to an unscrupulous abortionist for an illegal abortion, and died.

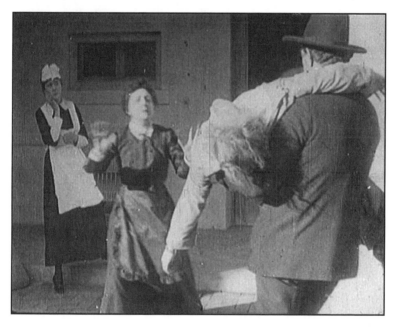

The librarian had observed my diligent efforts, and decided to pitch in and help.

I encourage you to nurture collegial relationships, not only for interviews and fundraising, but while doing research as well. Some of your most valuable results will come when you team up in your efforts.

When you set out to find information from other people, first ask yourself these questions: "Who knows about this subject?"

and then "Who cares about this subject?", finding out who shares your interest.

The answers to these two questions will point you toward people who probably have information you don't. They may live down the street or across the country. Sometimes you find people through referrals or word of mouth, sometimes on the Internet. You may decide to advertise in a newspaper to find people who worked at a certain company, or participated in a certain project. There is no one way to do this.

When you search for people, you will be looking for several categories.

People with Experience

Talk to people who have interacted with the material in some way or who know the characters in your film. Memories and stories add breadth and depth to a documentary.

Finding People

Documentary filmmaker David L. Brown found subjects for his film *Surfing for Life* by doing intense networking within the "mature" surfing community in Hawaii. He soon found several men who were still surfing in their seventies, eighties and nineties, but it took him nine months (with their help) to find three women who were still surfing after the age of fifty-five.

Surfing for Life (1999), David L. Brown.

In my series *Seeds of Hope*, I wanted to find commercial sex workers in Ethiopia. The only way to reach them and get interviews was through social workers in NGOs (non-governmental organizations) who had spent time building trust with them. We patiently communicated with one person after another, until we were finally successful. The result were hard-won, courageous interviews with sex workers, women who wanted to do whatever they could to prevent the spread of AIDS. They knew their lives were on the line, and decided that sharing their stories was a contribution they wanted to make.

People Who Study the Subject

Scholars may be excellent resources, but don't limit your search to professionals. Look for people who have made it their business or for whom it is their avocation or hobby to learn about the subject. Seek out collectors, fans, or even fanatics who may have boxes full of clippings, photographs, and other treasures.

Experts

In every field there are several people who know more about the subject than anyone else. If you arrange a meeting (by telephone, through the Internet, or in person) with any of these people, do as much research as possible before you talk to them.

A few of the people you talk to while doing research may become interviewees and/or advisors. Interesting documentaries often integrate informational interviews with more personal stories.

Gatekeepers

It may be difficult for a filmmaker to gain access to some experts (or an exclusive community) without first talking to a "gatekeeper," whose job it is to screen out most people who want to reach "their boss." Often gatekeepers are the only way to reach "well-protected" individuals.

For the film *Moment by Moment*, we had to call the assistant of a famous spinal cord injury doctor seven times before we could finally get through to his office.

Once we spoke with his assistant, and explained how the film would benefit spinal cord injury patients, it took another half dozen conversations before we succeeded in getting a riveting interview with the doctor. Winning over gatekeepers underscores the importance of building trust. The best approach is to present your project yourself. Self-promotion is an integral part of successful filmmaking, from research through distribution and publicity.

INFORMATION MANAGEMENT

Research can be a thrilling adventure, but it sometimes becomes a chore. One of the challenges of doing research is keeping up your interest. When you search endlessly for obscure facts, or have to plow through reams of densely written reports, research can become tedious. One of the ways to reduce the tedium and stress is to have a good information management system.

Creating an information management system that works for you is essential. If you don't have a good filing system, information quickly accumulates in piles, and soon you won't know what you have or where to find it.

A Simple Filing System

I use "file boxes" to start. I assign each project to a plastic crate and file each piece in a folder in the box as I go. If I can, I take the appropriate box with me when I do research on a particular subject. When others help with research, I can hand them the box. When we get information from the Internet, we download that, print out that and file it. Sometimes I ask people to e-mail concise summaries of their research, which I print and add to the box. Newspaper clippings, important lists — they all go into the box.

A Contact Database

You may talk to hundreds of people during the time that it takes to make your film. From the very first conversation, build a contact database to keep track of people — on paper, on 3x5 index cards, and/or on your computer.

Each person with whom you talk about the film should become part of a growing community. Some will have an interest in you and some in the film; some may offer connections for interviews; some may be potential donors; some may want a DVD when the project is done; some you may invite to feedback screenings or to the premiere. Some will help you promote the film when it is complete, or lend their support in other ways. Your network of connections is a treasure trove.

Frequently, you'll want to contact someone a second time to follow up on a conversation. Having an e-mail address or a phone number is necessary. (I am so sorry when I neglect to make a note and file or enter it, and need to reach someone again.)

Categories

Whether your database is electronic or on file cards, divide your contacts into categories so you can sort the names into groups.

For people who might be more important to the project, include more information than just the person's contact information. You might want to include notes of conversations, mutual connections, affiliations, and perhaps what they've published.

Every time you contact someone — whether by phone, e-mail, or in person — try to add a note to that person's file.

The Universal Matching Grant Service

There is a meta-benefit to doing good research. Once you "pay the entry fee" by doing your homework, reaching out to various communities, and organizing what you discover, you enhance the possibilities for connections between events and people. While some of these convergences may seem coincidental, others appear to be beyond chance. Many filmmakers feel they've entered a world of synchronicity. A string of uncanny coincidences may unfold as you shoot and edit your film. I experience this on every project. These moments more than outweigh the labor it takes to keep the project moving forward.

KEY POINTS

- To create a vibrant film, you need a genuine understanding of your subject.

- Background research is the process of immersing yourself in the subject of your documentary.

- Research continues throughout production.

- The kinds of resources you will use while doing background research include conversations, the Internet, books, articles, films, public documents, private documents, and more.

- Finding and talking to people is the one of the most fruitful parts of doing research.

- Set up a simple data management system at the beginning of your research.

- When you "pay your entry fee" by doing your homework, a Universal Matching Grant service seems to operate to help you reach your goal.

CHAPTER 4

BUILDING COMMUNITY: FROM KICKOFF TO LAUNCH

1. *When you commit to making a film, plan a kickoff meeting to help launch it.*

2. *A community of supporters can help you get the film right, get the film done, and get the film out.*

3. *An "interest group" attracts people who care about the film and/or you.*

4. *A "core group" is a small circle of people who are by your side for the whole journey — until the movie is complete.*

5. *If you can, create a trailer before the kickoff meeting.*

As soon as I commit to making a film, I plan a "kickoff meeting." This is a gathering where I lay out my vision, my goals, and my resources for a few people who are interested in the subject and perhaps already know my work. This gathering is an informal salon, where we crack a bottle of symbolic champagne on the bow of the film. My public declaration of intent literally launches the project. Making this commitment out loud lets the universe know I am serious!

By holding a kickoff meeting, you also tell *yourself* that this project is real. Making this "vow" to yourself, with witnesses, will help keep you going and give you momentum as your idea moves from fantasy to reality.

Among the hurdles to cross in making a documentary film are:

- Getting it right (aligning yourself with your own vision);

- Getting it done (working with a team);

- Getting it out (reaching viewers).

A supportive community will help you do all of these by reflecting your intention back to you.

They can help you *get the film "right"* through their ongoing feedback and suggestions.

They can help *get the film "done"* by volunteering, contributing time, helping you to raise money, and working with you to pull together other resources that you need to make the film.

They can help you *get the film "out in the world"* by being there when you launch it, and by showing it to others. Your community will create the first links in a chain of hands that might reach around the world.

Holding a Kickoff Meeting

The first thing to do is to set a date, and decide on a space. Choose someplace comfortable where you can serve light refreshments and talk with people. Most of my kickoff meetings have taken place in my own living room for less than twenty people. However, several times I brought together more than a hundred people for the kickoff.

Once you confirm a date and reserve a space, things are set into motion. Committing yourself publicly will also act as a spur to keep you going. The people who come will surely ask you every month or two, "So, when will the film be ready?"

You may wonder how you could hold a kickoff meeting before you have actually begun to make the film! The kickoff meeting is your statement to yourself and to the world that you are making a commitment and will follow through on the film project.

When you invite people to a kickoff meeting, explain that this is not a fundraising event. If a few guests offer to make a donation, acknowledge their interest, take their names, and tell them that you will talk to them soon, when you are ready to discuss financial details. (See Chapter 7 for a description of fundraising.)

Ideally, a kickoff meeting plants the seeds for a broad base of support later.

Getting Ready for the Kickoff Meeting

1. Prepare a simple one-sheet that gives an overview of the project, including your ideas for outreach and distribution to give to everyone who attends the meeting. People who want to learn more, to donate, or to volunteer, need this description to decide whether or not to get involved. Include an e-mail address and phone number for those who want more information.

2. If you have the time, inclination, and resources you might build a simple website describing your project. Even just a home page is helpful.

3. If you have some footage, from your own filming or another source, you might prepare a trailer, a short piece, no more than ten minutes, that gives your guests a sense of the project.

Making Your Presentation

Begin the meeting with an informal greeting. If the group is small enough, perhaps ask guests to introduce themselves. Once people are settled, if you have a trailer you could show that to start.

Trailers are usually between three and ten minutes long. When you create a trailer, be sure to use the strongest, best-shot images you have. Select footage that is compelling, and which communicates your vision.

The function of a trailer is to draw people in.

If you don't have any footage yet, you might want to do some shooting before the kickoff meeting. Before you make a trailer, it helps to write a treatment, to guide you. (See Chapter 6 for a description of treatments.)

After the trailer ends (if one is shown), speak candidly about why you chose this subject. Even if your presentation is understated, your passion is what will attract people to your work. Hearing you talk about your commitment is what will touch people. Just as "truth inspires passion" in the filmmaker, it will do so in others as well. Let the evening build as people are drawn into the project. If you have a vital idea, the film will start to have a life of its own. Encourage questions and answer these as fully as possible.

After the presentation, serve light refreshments. Having something to eat and drink is a way to let people know how much you appreciate their time.

Your Follow-Up

As the evening winds down, thank people for coming and make sure they give their names, phone, e-mail, etc. Possibly start to get commitments on a sign-up sheet. Invite people who want to work more closely with you and with the project to make a note of their desire to participate when they give their contact information. After closing the meeting formally, mingle with the people who are slower to leave. Some of them are still deciding whether or not to be involved.

Attracting a Support Group

Following the kickoff meeting, some of the people who attended will probably offer to help. Others who believe in what you doing will join these people as the project moves forward. They might volunteer their time and talents, make donations, organize screenings, and much more. I refer to people who want to help in these ways, and who are drawn together mainly by the content of the film, as an "interest group."

One of my most helpful interest group communities came together when I was producing a series of films on the AIDS epidemic in Ethiopia. At that point, I was overwhelmed by a hundred hours of interviews and meetings in a language I don't speak, Amharic. I was relieved and grateful when an Ethiopian faculty member at Stanford heard about the project, called, and asked if he could help.

I told him what I needed and he invited local Ethiopians to attend a small gathering where we they could see footage and discuss the project. A week later a dozen Ethiopians arrived for a kickoff meeting at my home. They included a radio producer, a social worker, a magazine publisher, several school teachers, and quite a few people from the computer industry — programmers, engineers, designers, and managers.

As they introduced themselves, I could see that what had seemed impossible was beginning to come together. Ethiopia was thousands of miles away, and yet here we were, in my living room, preparing to collaborate. I showed them footage we'd shot recently in Ethiopia.

They, in turn, talked about how helping was a way they could to do something about AIDS in Ethiopia. That night gave birth to a thriving interest group.

They — and another forty Ethiopian-Americans they helped recruit — became our colleagues in everything from translation to helping fill a thousand-person theater for the premiere of our series about AIDS in Ethiopia.

Your Interest Group

Your strongest pool of volunteer support will usually come from the communities most affected by your film.

With *Why Do These Kids Love School?* I had dozens of people with progressive, alternative views on education that helped me in every way. For *Motherhood by Choice*, the reproductive rights activists from across the country were by my side, all the way.

I was able to complete the film *Woman by Woman* (filmed in India with interviews in Hindi) by attracting a group of East Indian volunteers living in the San Francisco Bay Area who translated and transcribed dozens of Hindi interviews. When I needed perspectives on the subtleties of what the Indian villagers were communicating, I asked those who had lived in villages to watch the work-in-progress and give me feedback. They gave us invaluable candid suggestions, and carefully alerted us to be sensitive about certain cultural taboos.

Members of the interest group may be part of the community you are documenting (as the Indians and Ethiopians were), or because the topic of your film addresses a subject they care about (with the reproductive rights activists). Sometimes they are simply friends who want to be involved in what you are doing. When the time comes to publicize screening events, the people who have been helping on the films are the first to buy seats, and sell tickets to their communities.

Your Core Group

During production, some of the people in the interest group may want to make a deeper commitment to you and to the project, They join you in your journey, and stay with you until the end! These people are ideal candidates for what I call a "core group." (See Chapter 8, Your Core Group.)

The core group is your "inner circle" of people who will be by your side — emotionally and practically — throughout the project. Core group members may work with you on a daily basis on the production, or they may just hold your hand by phone and e-mail. My friends Dania and Marilyn became part of a core group for my first film on women's rights. At the beginning of the project, they both sent letters — without my asking — to their own friends and family, inviting people from their circles to contribute to the film. Together they raised enough to do the first several shoots. They saw what I was doing, and offered to help.

Five years later, when the third and final film in the women's rights series premiered at the Palace of Fine Arts in San Francisco, Dania and Marilyn were among the first to RSVP to the big-ticket special reception before the screening. *That* kind of loyalty is what a core group provides — people who support you all the way!

COMMUNITY

A variety of people will come and go as the project continues — good friends might help out when they can, family members you know you can count on will show up when you need them, fellow filmmakers, crewmembers, interns, or some of your volunteers are there, some for a day, some for years.

It is physically possible for a filmmaker to "go it alone," but that doesn't seem to be best way to make a movie. Most of us need and somehow put together a collaborative community of people who, in different ways at different times, become a team.

KEY POINTS

- Three of the main challenges to making a documentary film are getting it right, getting it done, and getting it out.

- A supportive community will help you do these things.

- Before holding the kickoff meeting, consider preparing a trailer that communicates your vision.

- A kickoff meeting is where you commit yourself, publicly, to producing and finishing the film. Making this commitment lets the universe know you are serious! This affirmation at the beginning helps give you the energy and support to finish the film.

- From the beginning of your project, invest some of your time in building and sustaining a community that can grow with the film.

CHAPTER 5

Planning an Unscripted Documentary

1. *Many documentaries are unscripted.*

2. *An unscripted documentary will develop as you work.*

3. *There are various distinct "styles" of documentary. You can choose one of these styles, or combine them.*

4. *A straightforward way to get started on a film: Clarify what you want your film to be about, write a brief overview, decide what you want to shoot, and begin shooting.*

5. *Shooting without a script does not mean grabbing the camera and running out to shoot whatever you see. It means planning thoughtfully and being open to the story that emerges from the material.*

Some filmmakers prepare a script, treatment, and proposal before beginning to shoot. My approach is different. I usually do some background research, make contacts with crew and interviewees, start filming, and then allow the story to emerge from the footage. I gather material and raise money as I go.

This chapter suggests ways to start your film before you know exactly where you will end up, and encourages you not to worry about how you are going to get there.

Do You Need a Script?

One of the first decisions you will make is whether or not you will write a script. Many modern documentaries are made without scripts. Scripted documentaries, however, have a long and prestigious history.

Scripted Documentaries

Some documentaries — such as most educational and industrial films — call for a clear structure and a script.

One of the best examples of a scripted documentary is *Night Mail*, a film made in 1936 by Harry Watt and Basil Wright.

Night Mail shows the nightly mail trains between England and Scotland. A voice-over narration, written by W. H. Auden, tells how the mail service delivers mail each night to towns and villages.

A combination of great camera work, strong images, poetic narration, and compelling music made the film an instant success.

Night Mail (1936), Harry Watt and Basil Wright.

There are many good books that address scripted documentaries, and one of the best is *Directing the Documentary* by Michael Rabiger.

But — for the kind of documentary that this book invites you to dare to make — what you need more than a script is a sense of adventure.

The Power of Unscripted Moments

The key to success when working without a script is to be ready for moments that become the heart of the story. After deciding to make a film about an innovative school, my videographer, Peter, and I chose to spend the first day in the schoolyard, ready to record whatever happened.

The first day of filming, Peter waded into a group of twenty nursery school students. Soon the children forgot about the camera. He filmed as they screamed with excitement, dunking fat brushes into cans of paint, bristles dripping with thick wet color as they painted their climbing equipment, and sometimes each other.

I didn't need to tell Peter what to shoot. He knew, intuitively, how to spot "the action." I watched as he followed a little boy with golden curls who was starting to cry. The child ran over to his teacher to tell her he was sad. She leaned toward him to listen.

As Peter came closer, the camera microphone picked up the little boy's words, "John splashed paint in my ear."

The teacher asked, "Did you tell him you didn't like it?" The boy shook his head "No," then turned toward the other little boy, who was now far across the schoolyard. Peter followed as the boy toddled over to the other child.

We picked up his voice as he announced, with determination, "John! Don't splash paint in my ear!" There is no way we could have scripted that moment. Did we have great sound? No. Was it good enough to capture a great moment? Yes.

Later, during an interview with the director of the school, she said, "We don't label children's behavior as good or bad, we look at what's working and what isn't working, and that makes sense to kids." Her statement explains why no one was reprimanded in the paint-splashing episode.

To film an unscripted documentary, you decide generally what to film — the time of day, the location, who to interview — and prepare to shoot that material. Then you let the story unfold. In this case a scene was built around one unplanned exchange that tells a story about this alternative approach to education. Ideally, the footage and the emerging story "click." (See Chapter 15 for a description of editing.)

Be alert for opportunities to shape the story so it is yours. First, you choose what to shoot, and then you select the moments that stand out for you.

The absence of a blueprint does not mean grabbing the camera and running out to shoot whatever you see. Instead, it means beginning early on to put together a supportive team; doing some homework first; finding and framing the idea; doing background research; and once you start shooting, opening yourself to the direction suggested by what you see and hear. In this way, you allow what you gather to inform you about where to go instead of following a predetermined script.

Working in this way, I find that the script begins to develop as I work. Each interviewee adds direction while the new footage and other images suggest more to the story. I bring these pieces into the editing process where the script takes shape.

YOUR TREATMENT

A treatment (for a documentary film) is usually one to three pages that overview the project in a narrative form, as a short, detailed story (with a beginning, a middle, and an end) describing what the audience will see on the screen. If you are writing it for yourself, which is useful, it should be one of the first things you do. However, some filmmakers wait until they approach funders and use the treatment as a frame for others to better understand what you are planning to do. As you go forward, for some potential funders, you may need to write a much longer treatment. Eventually, you will write a full proposal.

You can use your treatment as a springboard to write a proposal, create a budget, raise money, and do preproduction planning. It will help you estimate out how many locations, shooting days, and interviewees you might need to make your film.

Ideally, a treatment will pull the reader in immediately, creating interest, and a desire to read all the way to the end. Make your treatment concise, yet detailed. The details will engage the reader, and help you to figure out how to "flesh out" your film.

At this point, you might review how other filmmakers have solved problems similar to ones you face. As you work on your treatment, you can combine previous approaches with your own, and come up with new ways to use the elements you have to work with.

You might begin your treatment by describing an interesting event, anecdote, or scene. Tell the reader what he or she will see onscreen as the event plays out. When you have a compelling opening, tell the rest of the story in a way that will hold a reader from beginning to end. As you write, keep in mind that the treatment is only a rough sketch of what your film might look like. The final story will be decided in the editing room.

Ways to Tell Your Story

Once you are clear whether or not you will have a script, the question becomes: What filmmaking style will be yours?

In film school, students usually learn different styles of documentary filmmaking. Then, when they set out to make a film, they choose the appropriate style.

But as long as you are familiar with the major styles as options, you may choose one style, and stay with it through the film, or you may mix styles as the material demands. As you discover your own style, you might watch documentaries made in different styles, and choose one or more that feel right for you and your films.

Some Styles Used by Documentary Filmmakers

In his book *Introduction to Documentary*, Bill Nichols defines five distinct styles of documentary:

- The Filmmaker as Poet
- The Filmmaker as Teacher
- The Filmmaker as Observer
- The Filmmaker as a Participant
- The Filmmaker as Performer

Let's look at several these major "styles" of documentaries:

As Poet

In the poetic documentary, you record images and sounds, and reassemble them into a visual and audio "symphony." There isn't any central character, except perhaps the locality or subject. Examples include: *Koyaanisqatsi* (1983), by Godfrey Reggio, and *Berlin, Song of a City* (1928), by Walter Ruttman. The strength of this style is its capacity to capture the *gestalt* of a time, place, or person. The risk is that the film can become too abstract for the viewer to follow.

As Teacher

When you make a teaching or "expository" documentary, you set out to convey information. Early examples of this style used an authoritative "voice of God" narrator. Examples include:

Why We Fight (1942-1945) by Frank Capra, or *The Plow That Broke the Plains* (1936) by Pare Lorenz. The strength of this approach is its capacity to convey information. The risk is that the narrative may become didactic.

As Observer

When you act as the "observer" you become a "fly on the wall" and capture the reality of daily life. Examples include: *Don't Look Back* (1967) by D.A. Pennebaker, or *Salesman* (1969) by Albert and David Maysles. The strength of this style is that it provides a venue for profound insights into the people and events being filmed. The risk is showing situations out of context without background or history. Sometimes, as when Frederick Wiseman filmed inmates in a mental hospital without their consent in *Titicut Follies* (1969), the filmmaker risks being criticized as being exploitive.

As Participant

When you interact with the world you are filming, you may be on-camera as a participant in the film, or off-camera as an interviewer. Examples include: *Sherman's March* (1986) by Ross McElwee, or *Roger and Me* (1989) by Michael Moore.

The strength of this style is that it can preserve history through interviews and archival sources. The risk is relying on the story told by the people being interviewed (which may or may not be accurate), and intruding into people's lives.

As Performer

You may choose to become an actor in your film in an attempt to communicate the essence of your own experience. You might use music, poetry, dance, or enacted scenes to express yourself. An example is *Tongues Untied* (1989) by Marlon Riggs. The strength of this style is that it shows the world the subjective reality of your experience from inside your world.

The risk is that the film may feel narcissistic.

Must-See Documentaries

One of the best ways to learn about different styles of film-making is to watch classic films. Filmmaker Aronn Ranen has compiled an excellent list of must-see documentaries at *http://dvworkshops.com.*

GETTING STARTED

When I hold a filmmaking workshop, people ask, "If I don't have a script, where do I start?"

Begin with an Overview

A simple way to begin is to write a one-sheet description of your project (which might actually be your "treatment," as well as you understand it at that point). It won't be perfect or final, but this way you can set the process into motion. On this sheet, sketch the themes, the story, the characters, and what you think will be your approach. This overview creates a jumping off place for an unscripted documentary.

With overview in hand, ask yourself:

- Whom do I want to interview?

- What locations do I want to visit and perhaps shoot?

- What activities do I want to capture?

- What research do I need to do?

The story — with this approach — will evolve from the material as you shoot, view the footage, do more research, and get feedback from other people.

Without a script, you need to know the direction you hope to go, loosen the reins, and let the interviewees and other footage get you there. The original idea and your project description together, will serve as a compass.

Decide What to Shoot

You have an idea that appeals to you. Now is the time to brainstorm the people, places, and situations that you envision could tell the story.

➥ Whom would you like to interview?

Think generously of people you might talk with. Make lists of whomever comes to mind. Some may be friends, and some may be strangers. You do not even need to know names. You can simply list them by position or title.

Name people who you think will know whatever you want someone to talk about. Don't be shy, just free associate. As you make this list, choose people who intrigue you or who are experts. Be bold.

Add to your list "the best authorities in the field." Even if you don't interview these people, you will still need to know who they are. You may want to read their books, articles, or writings they've posted on the Internet.

Include famous people, even if you don't think there's a chance in the world that they'd have the time or interest to talk to you. You never know. One of the people on my wish list for my current project about election integrity is Congressman John Conyers, who may know more about election reform than anyone in the country. In preparation, I am learning about him on the Internet and reading a book he wrote about irregularities in the 2004 presidential election. I may or may not interview him, or he might become a valuable advisor.

➥ Where would you like to shoot?

List the locations and landmarks that seem essential to your idea, as well as places that excite you. In every film, there are places that define the characters and the story. If you can film these places, they will give your film depth and power.

In *Man of Aran* (1934), Robert Flaherty used the turbulent sea and rocky coasts of the Isle of Aran to define the lives of the people who lived on the island. The stark beauty of the island illustrated the strength and spirit of the people who lived there. The inhabitants survived in a place so bleak that even soil had to be created by backbreaking labor.

☞ What situations or events would you like to document?

What is a situation? Think about the activities the people in your documentary do as they go through their daily lives.

As you list situations that might be filmed, give some thought to the sequences of events. In *Man of Aran*, Flaherty films a whale hunt. He also films all the events leading up to the hunt, the preparation of the boat, the coiling of the line, the preparation of the harpoon, and then the climactic killing of the whale.

Think about mundane tasks such as going to market, or drinking a cup of tea.

Consider events that happen once a year, like a birthday, or once in a lifetime, like a wedding or a graduation.

When you make a list of these situations, certain ones with the most "life" will rise to the top.

If possible, try to find situations of cinematic power, where conflict is revealed. Conflict is the heart of drama, and will capture the audience's interest. Look for situations where the conflict is visual. During the filming of a lively fifth-grade soccer game, a fight erupted over fairness. In the final cut, I showed just a clip of the shouting match to show that this problem could not be solved with a quick apology. The scene dissolves to a meeting the next day, where the students discuss what happened and brainstorm ways to head off the problem next time.

Making an Unscripted Documentary Is an Act of Trust

With an unscripted documentary, rather than planning everything beforehand, you simply give yourself guidelines which let the story evolve based on the material. If you do your research and have a sense of the story you want to tell before you start shooting, you allow yourself to be open to surprises, making changes as you go.

If you allow interviewees to "free associate" they are more likely to share ideas that feel alive to them. Open-ended interviews often lead to those moments in a film you couldn't possibly have scripted!

In *Moment by Moment,* Jeramy describes his once a week overnight stays in the hospital when his wife, Molly, was still wearing a cage-like metal "halo" that immobilized her head and spinal cord.

"How do you make love to your wife in this cage? It was overwhelming. It was a kind of a surreal experience but we were intimate in the way that we could be and that was really important for both of us."

How could anyone have scripted that! I had no idea people with severe spinal cord injury could have sex in the hospital under the cover of night! That personal remembrance came out of a free-flowing interview. Later, in the edit room, we were able to cut together a whole scene based on them rebuilding their sexual connection after the injury.

By deciding beforehand what you want to have happen, you run the risk of missing what may turn out to be the best material!

KEY POINTS

- You can produce a documentary without a script.

- Shooting without a script requires planning thoughtfully first.

- Some unscripted documentaries require extensive research and preparation before shooting begins.

- When you shoot an unscripted documentary, the final story is built as you shoot, and in the editing room after shooting is complete, not on a word processor before filming begins.

- Summarize the stages of your preproduction by writing a detailed treatment as part of your planning process.

CHAPTER 6

Creating a Blueprint for Your Film

A well-written proposal is a blueprint for your film that will help you:

1. *Visualize your film, from preproduction through distribution.*

2. *Create a realistic, workable budget.*

3. *Raise funds for the project.*

4. *Attract experienced crew and advisors.*

5. *Organize your information.*

The elements of a standard proposal are described in this chapter.

Although the prospect of writing a proposal may seem daunting, keep in mind that a proposal will help you to visualize your whole film, from preproduction to distribution.

Writing a detailed proposal will highlight challenges that may have been invisible to you at first. If you think you want to talk to your Senator about environmental reform, do you know if he or she will he agree to an interview? And, if so, and you need to fly to D.C., how much will it cost? Lodging? Food? As you lay out your budget, you may see you can't handle that expense. Maybe you could talk to your local county supervisor instead. The supervisor may be delighted to be interviewed. That is an example of the kind of consideration that writing a proposal can reveal early on, when you can still modify your plans.

Your Proposal

A comprehensive, well-researched proposal will help guide the film through preproduction, production, postproduction, outreach, and distribution. Researching and writing a thorough proposal demands that you summarize your story, its themes, the dramatic structure, and categories of potential interviewees. In addition, most proposals call for a plan which lays out how you plan for the film to reach people.

Theoretically, a proposal would anticipate everything. But the reality of documentary filmmaking is that you simply can't plan everything in advance. So, once again, you do the best you can, keeping in mind that discovery is an integral part of documentary filmmaking.

WHY YOU NEED A PROPOSAL

You need a proposal for several reasons, not the least of which is that a well-written proposal helps to give your project a focus. Clarity is difficult to envision without going through the process of breaking down the parts.

To Focus the Project

All the research that you do for a proposal can be used again, for press releases, newspaper stories, magazine articles, and other grant applications. Once you have taken the time to put together a good proposal, and prepare to submit it to funders, the universe seems to "know" that the proposal is out there. Soon after writing a proposal for *Why Do These Kids Love School?* I was making copies of it in a local copy shop.

A woman who had several children in one of the schools I hoped to document approached me and asked, "What are copying?" I explained the project to her and she asked for a copy of the proposal to take home and read.

Soon after that meeting, we received a check for $5,000 from her family foundation.

Fundraising

Organizations that donate money to media makers usually need to see a proposal before they make a grant. Proposals come in different lengths. A small foundation that makes grants in a limited geographic area may only want a letter with a short project description and a one-page budget. A national organization, like the National Endowment for the Humanities (NEH), may require a 150-page book. Individuals may or may not want to see a proposal.

Recruiting Your Team

A good proposal can be used to attract experts on your subject or experienced filmmakers to your project. A well-written, fleshed-out proposal will help convince people, including potential funders, that you are serious.

ELEMENTS OF A PROPOSAL

You can use this template to write a basic proposal. A basic proposal can be shortened or lengthened, depending on the requirements of the foundation. A proposal usually contains most or all these elements:

- Cover letter (personalized for each individual who will receive the proposal)
- Cover page
- Table of contents
- Introduction or project summary
- Treatment or project description
- Intended audience

- Production plan and time line

- Key personnel

- Funding strategy

- Distribution plan

- Budget

- Non-profit fiscal sponsor 501(c)(3) letter

Cover Letter

The cover letter should be one page long, or less. Include:

- Name of the project or film

- Your name and contact information (address, phone number, e-mail, website address)

- The name and address of the person to whom you are addressing the proposal

- A brief statement of your purpose in sending the proposal ("We are seeking completion funds for a documentary on wildlife refuges in Botswana.")

- A brief statement why this proposal meets the foundation's purpose ("This documentary is in keeping with your commitment to support the establishment of wildlife refuges in Africa.")

- A statement of thanks to the person to whom it is addressed for considering your proposal

Cover Page

Create a simple cover page to be used with every copy of the proposal. Even if your proposal is short, do create a cover page for it which includes:

- The name of the project and/or the documentary

- Your name and contact information (address, phone number, e-mail, website address)

- The name of your 501(c)(3) sponsor (if your company is not a non-profit) or your own non-profit company

- Depending on the foundation, you might include a compelling image taken from your footage

Table of Contents

Every proposal benefits from a table of contents, especially if the proposal is longer than ten pages.

Introduction

An engaging introduction may prove to be the most important page in the entire proposal. You want it to be a magnet that draws the reader in with curiosity to learn more about the project. A well-crafted paragraph at the beginning of the narrative description should give the reader a reason to continue to read the rest of the document. Include a statement of why this project is important and, if appropriate, the need it will fulfill. If the project is timely, explain why the film should be made within a certain time period.

Treatment

The body of the proposal contains the basic story in treatment form. (A treatment is a narrative summary that lets the reader "see" and "hear" how the film will play.) Try to include one or more compelling stories that hook the reader immediately.

Woven into the treatment should be a general description of the approach you plan to take, and the general content of the film.

You might say for example whether you plan to shoot *cinéma vérité* in which the camera acts as a silent witness to people's lives, or "essay" style with interviews and voice-over narration. If you can characterize your film as "balanced journalism" or "responsible advocacy," you will stand a better chance with most foundations.

Intended Audience

For whom is the movie being made? Who will buy tickets to a screening, purchase DVDs, tune into broadcasts, or order copies for their library?

Include a concise description of the intended audience with as many specifics as possible: ages, education levels, economic status, geographical locations, and a short explanation of why certain populations would be interested in your film.

Production Plan

In this section, include your intended schedule for research, preproduction, production, and postproduction. Most foundations realize that the time line will probably change. A time line for a broadcast quality thirty-minute documentary should give estimates for the following steps, usually estimated in weeks:

- Research and fundraising

- Preproduction

- Production

- Postproduction

Funders will look at your production plan (and budget) to see if the project is realistic and the goals are attainable. They will recognize if you exaggerate, underestimate, or misstate the facts. Your best path is to do the necessary research, state the facts, and stay with conservative estimates.

Personnel

List the principal people who you hope will be working on the project, and include a short biography for each person. If you are a first-time filmmaker, it is very helpful to have an experienced co-producer or executive producer, director of photography, and/or editor.

Early drafts of the proposal can help recruit these seasoned people and then their names can be incorporated into the next version of the proposal.

Funding

Describe a multi-pronged strategy for funding the film. List whomever you plan to approach: the foundations, corporations, organizations, and categories of people you will contact. Discuss any plans for house parties of other fundraisers.

Note the money you have already raised (including in-kind donations) and your plans for raising the balance. Most funders want to be assured that they will not be the only source of money.

Distribution

Many funders require the inclusion of distribution plans before they fund a film. Foundations and donors have learned from experience that there must be a clear plan for how to get a finished film out into the world. Demonstrate that you know how to get the film to the intended viewers, to your potential funders.

Your distribution plan should include a website, and possibly a discussion guide. If appropriate, the plan might target festivals, educational institutions, libraries, community organizations, activist groups, as well as broadcasters such as PBS, cable, network, and foreign TV markets.

Budget

Attach an estimated budget for your film, following the distribution plan. (See Chapter 7 for a description of budget-writing.)

Attachments

Attach a non-profit fiscal sponsor support letter and/or a 501(c)(3) letter from the IRS. You may or may not need both.

A non-profit fiscal sponsor is able to receive and disburse tax deductible donations for your project. (See Chapter 7 for a description of non-profit fiscal sponsors.)

A 501(c)(3) letter is a standard IRS letter that non-profit organizations give to donors. This may be about your own group or from a sponsor. The letter says the donor is legally entitled to a tax deduction for his or her contribution.

Attach other documents as needed. These documents might include letters of support from users, potential distributors and broadcasters, reviews and articles about key players in your documentary.

Proposal Writing Resources

Finding the right proposal and grant writing resources can be daunting. Even a cursory search of the Internet will reveal hundreds of resources (including books, articles, and websites) that explain grant and proposal writing. This short section on resources will get you started.

Funder Guidelines

When you are writing a proposal, the first place to look is the funder's own proposal-writing guidelines.

Most foundations and organizations that provide grants have proposal writing guidelines on their websites. Print a copy, *and follow the guidelines exactly* when you write a proposal for the organization.

Existing Resources

Film Arts Foundation

Non-profit filmmakers' organizations (like the Film Arts Foundation at *http://www.filmarts.org/home.php*) sometimes keep copies of proposals written by their members in a lending library.

The Foundation Center

The Foundation Center at *http://fdncenter.org/* is a national organization with proposal writing seminars, proposal advice, online databases of funders, and online copies of recently awarded grants.

The resources at the Foundation Center include:

A free proposal writing tutorial and The Foundation Center Proposal Writing Short Course, at *http://fdncenter.org/learn/ shortcourse/prop1.html.*

The Foundation Directory Online Plus is an online service with two databases — the first contains the ten thousand largest U.S. foundations and the second contains half a million recently awarded grants. You can subscribe to the service for $29.95 per month at *http://fconline.fdncenter.org.*

Books

Shaking the Money Tree by Morrie Warshawski (*www.mwp .com*) is a classic book on fundraising.

Writing, Directing and Producing Documentary Films and Videos by Alan Rosenthal. An easy to read account of directing, writing, and producing documentary films.

The Independent Film and Video Maker's Guide by Michael Wiese (*www.mwp.com*). An excellent, practical, and easy to read guide to independent filmmaking.

KEY POINTS

- A comprehensive, well-written proposal will help guide the film through early research, preproduction, production, postproduction, outreach, and distribution.

- A proposal will help you raise money and recruit experienced filmmakers and possibly advisors.

- The introduction should capture the reader's attention immediately.

- The body tells the story of your film in treatment form. Include a brief description of the content and the intended style of the film.

- The first place to look for proposal writing help is the potential funder's proposal writing guidelines.

- When submitting a proposal to any organization, *follow the organization's proposal writing guidelines exactly.*

CHAPTER 7

ATTRACTING FUNDING

1. *People give money to people, not projects.*

2. *Every film requires some funding, and that money has to be raised.*

3. *Don't be shy to ask for money. You are giving potential donors the opportunity to help bring something important into the world.*

4. *Assure donors that their money will be well-invested.*

5. *Use existing resources (books, sample budgets, other filmmakers) to get perspective and create a realistic budget before you begin fundraising.*

The most important piece in the fundraising puzzle is this — *people give money to people, not projects.* When you make a commitment to raise money, you take on a mission, which is to communicate your vision wherever you go. You need to bring your enthusiasm for the project into conversations with potential funders, and potential funders are everywhere. The challenge is to let people know, wherever you go, that contributing to your film is an opportunity to invest in something that will make a difference. It is your vision which will attract donors.

RAISING SPIRITS

Filmmaking can be a very expensive art form, but it doesn't have to be. If you get people to donate services and find ways to cut expenses, it's possible to make a ten-minute documentary for less than two thousand dollars. At the other end of the spectrum, a fully funded hour-long broadcast piece for public television might easily cost well over a million dollars by the time it's ready for distribution.

Whether you are funding your work out of pocket, getting donations, or working with a PBS station, the money to make a film has to come from somewhere. Having your own digital editing system will lower your costs significantly, but making a film is never free.

Asking for contributions may be difficult at first.

You'll need to ask yourself about how you handle money in general: Do I know how to budget money wisely? Am I overly cautious, and do I find it difficult to spend money, even when necessary? Issues with financial management that have haunted you in the past may surface when you start to ask people for money. If managing money has been challenging for you in the past, invite someone you trust to work with you on fundraising.

First-time filmmakers often feel as if they are begging when they ask for money. Don't be apologetic. Remember you are giving people an opportunity. As a filmmaker, you have the ability to create something which gives voice to peoples' concerns and addresses their issues. They will invest in you because they believe that through your film you can bring *their* voices to the world. Bottom line is they will be funding you to do that for them.

PEOPLE FUND PEOPLE, NOT IDEAS

It is crucial to bring your unique vision and spirit to the task of fundraising. Ideas are abstract, you are real!

When potential donors meet you, or read your proposal, they will be asking themselves, "Does this person have the drive and integrity to bring this project to the finish line? Will my money be well invested?"

Potential donors will have plenty of other opportunities for giving. Your challenge is to show them that you, and your project, are good choices for their donation.

The first question many donors ask is, "Will this person be able to complete and distribute this film?" When people donate money to your project, they are underwriting your willingness and ability to do the work. They need to feel that investing in you will be "profitable" or, at a minimum, relatively safe.

Donors always hope that the completed work will reach a significant audience. The distribution section of the all-important proposal will show them that you have a plan for getting your film out in the world. Some donors might turn to the distribution section before reading anything else in the proposal. (See Chapter 6 for a description of proposal writing.)

Another way you can increase your chances of being funded is by recruiting or attracting good advisors for your project — before you begin fundraising. Add the advisors' names to your proposal, and when you talk to potential donors, let them know that these people will be helping you and that you are ready to take advice from experienced people.

When I set out to fund a film, I don't set out to "raise money," as much as I set out to raise trust. I tell potential donors, "Here is why I believe in this, here is what I've done so far, and here's my vision for where I will take this." Funders will begin to feel their own connection to your project through your passion.

Friends of friends (people I'd never met before) expressed an interest in funding one of my films. They invited me to meet with them. I remember the day vividly. They lived in a large stucco house with a wide veranda, a barn for their horses — and a beautiful ballroom. I arrived with a briefcase filled with paper — reviews of my past work, a budget, a treatment — and no idea what to expect.

When I arrived I didn't know that they had already decided to contribute a set amount. Their planned donation would cover our costs for making copies of the film, submitting it to festivals, and sending it out for reviews.

As we chatted, seated on facing couches, I realized that what they wanted from me was not in my briefcase and was not on paper (though I was glad I had brought those things). They wanted to hear my vision for the film. I set aside the papers I'd brought, and told them, with conviction, what I hoped to accomplish. They listened, and after I was done, they spoke quietly with each other. He took out his checkbook, turned toward her, she nodded.

I learned later that, as a result of my visit, they doubled the amount they'd planned to give. I experienced in that meeting what I now know to be true in every encounter with funders: You need to have your facts and figures ready, but your passion for your own project is the most important part of your proposal.

REALISTIC BUDGETING

One of the necessary steps in most fundraising efforts is to lay out an accurate budget. I say most, because sometimes people will simply give you money without a budget. That happens rarely, but now and then it does happen. Usually, you need to lay out in some detail what things will cost. Fortunately, there is nothing mysterious about making a good budget.

A sensible first step might be to read *Film and Video Budgets* by Michael Wiese and Deke Simon (*www.mwp.com*). This book contains sample budgets and detailed explanations of individual line items.

The key to creating a realistic, workable budget is making sure that you include all relevant line items, and getting accurate, current numbers. Find out what things really cost. If you don't know, find out. You might need to call several sources or do a web search to get the best deal.

A Book that Shows All the Gear
Dream Gear: Cool and Innovative Tools for Film, Video, and TV Professionals by Catherine Lorenze (*www.mwp.com*)

A Few Places to Get Realistic Prices for Gear
Abel CineTech *www.abelcine.com*
B&H Photo Video *www.bhphotovideo.com*
TapeWorks Texas *www.tapeworkstexas.com/*
Video Guys *www.videoguys.com/*
Zotz Digital *http://www.zotzdigital.com/*

EUROPE
Production Gear UK *www.productiongear.co.uk/*

CANADA
DV Café *www.dvshop.ca/dvcafe.html*

COMPARISON SHOPPING WEBSITES
Nextag.com *www.nextag.com*
BizRate.com *www.bizrate.com*

LOCAL SERVICES
For local services, you usually need to make phone calls.

Many donors, especially foundations, know what things should cost. If certain figures seem inflated or too low, donors may be suspicious of your whole proposal.

Always Work with Reputable Dealers
When buying expensive video production equipment, always buy from reputable dealers. A reputable dealer will deliver exactly what you ordered, promptly. Most will allow you to return the equipment within a few days if you get the equipment and learn that it does not meet your needs.

If a price on the Web looks "too good to be true," it probably is. There are — sadly — many shady operations on the Web that offer super-low prices as a way to hook unwary filmmakers. After you give them your money, the equipment may arrive late, broken, or without a manufacturer's warranty.

Also, inevitably, if you set your sights too low and under-budget, you will almost always end up spending your own money to make up the difference. The truth is, many filmmakers end up spending their own money to complete their films, no matter what they do, but that is another subject. Under-budgeting will make the situation even more difficult.

With a realistic budget, you will know how much it should take to make the movie and you are less likely to over-spend. When your budget is in good order, you will be able to show potential donors that you know what it takes to get the movie done.

Steps to a Realistic Budget

1. Write a treatment. Then use the treatment to estimate shooting days, locations, interviewees, travel, research, and postproduction costs.

2. Double-check, and make sure your budget includes everything you will need.

3. Research a range of current rates for equipment and services.

4. Check in with one or more experienced filmmakers. An experienced filmmaker will spot omissions and errors immediately. Correct these errors before you show your budget to a funder.

Crafting the Budget

The first step in crafting a budget is to do a "treatment breakdown."

1. Go through your treatment and highlight locations, interviewees, and vérité scenes. (Vérité scenes are those scenes where the camera and camera crew follow the action, blend with the background, and become as "a fly on the wall.")

2. Estimate the total number of "shooting days" you will need to go to all the locations and shoot the footage you want.

3. Estimate your travel costs.

4. Estimate the time required for preproduction. How many days will it take to do to background research, pre-interviewing, and preproduction planning?

5. Estimate the time required for logging footage and transcribing interviews. For every hour of footage that you shoot, figure three hours for logging. For every hour of interviews that you choose to transcribe, figure three hours of transcription time.

6. Estimate the time required for postproduction. (See Chapter 6, Writing a Proposal, Production Plan and Time Line.)

Accurate Line Items

Get realistic rates for crew, equipment, and services. When you write your budget, I suggest you consider noting professional documentary rates, as well as possible lower negotiated rates. For example, an experienced Director of Photography who charges $1,000 a day for a commercial project might agree to do your project for $400 a day if he or she believes in the subject. You might comment on that range in your budget with a note.

Include a salary for yourself, and make it realistic. You may not draw this salary, but it is important to add it as a line item.

If you don't have the right equipment for the project, instead of renting it, you might plan to buy the equipment and rent it to the production at the going rate.

The Non-Profit "Umbrella"

Foundations are generally required to make grants through another non-profit organization; private individuals often prefer to make donations through a non-profit so their donations will be tax-deductible.

There are several ways to work this out. One is to work with an existing non-profit organization, which will act as a "conduit" or "sponsor" for contributions, sometimes referred to as "umbrella." A second way is to create a non-profit 501(c)(3) organization for your work.

For your first films, I recommend working through an existing non-profit, which receives funds from donors and foundations and disburses that money to you. For their services, the handling fee is usually between 4% and 8%.

Forming your own non-profit corporation may take several months, and might cost a thousand dollars or more. There are also online sites that walk you through the process, for a much smaller fee. Most filmmakers who've formed non-profits wait until they've made a few films before taking on that responsibility. At first, your time, attention, and money should go into filmmaking — not into setting up and running a small corporation. As your budgets grow, and your work becomes known, you may then decide to set up a non-profit for your work.

FUNDRAISING OPTIONS

Money to support independent filmmaking comes from a variety of sources. These might include:

Friends and Family

Initial funding often comes from the people closest to you. If you decide to approach friends and family members, set up an informal one-to-one meeting, at home or perhaps in a small restaurant for lunch or coffee. Before the meeting, be sure to let the other person know you will be discussing funding your project at the meeting. In some cases, they might end up advising you, and making suggestions, but not making a donation. These non-monetary contributions are valuable, and should be treated as a gift — a different kind of gift.

House Parties

Those who accept an invitation to come to a fundraising house party understand that they will be asked to support the project with a donation. Sometimes you will show guests a few minutes of the work in progress. This event might be at your house, or the home of one of your friends, or in any comfortable, small room in a convenient building like a library or community center. It is a good idea to give guests a range of options for donations.

(See Chapter 4 for a description of kickoff meetings, which you can adapt for fundraising.)

Mailings

Mailings work best if you send brief, targeted communications to people with whom you already have a relationship. In a mailing, bulleted requests that highlight specific needs usually work better than a general "ask." A strong image from the film helps to capture the recipient's attention. Plan to include a personal note that is clearly addressed to that individual or family. On the whole, I have found that larger general mailings tend to bring disappointingly low results.

Foundation Grants

Your project may or may not be appropriate for a larger foundation grant. Foundations generally give larger sums ($50,000 and above) to bigger budget projects. There are smaller foundations that do give more modest grants ($1,000 to $10,000) to smaller projects, and you can find them through a Foundations Center *http://fconline.fdncenter.org/* search. Obviously, these are not strict rules. Look at previous grants from each likely foundation, and make your choices depending on your project and their interests.

Credit Card

We've all heard about (or know) filmmakers who max out their credit cards to make a film. The hope is that the film will make money, and pay off the credit card debt! In reality, filmmakers who make movies on credit cards usually end up with a year or more of a debt that they pay off with income from other sources.

Don't Make Your Film on Credit Cards

After watching first-time filmmakers reach for their credit cards, and never get their money back, my advice is: Ask for donations, cut corners wherever you can, spend your own money if you must, but do not go into credit card debt to make your film.

Your Own Money

Inevitably, you will be tempted to put some of your own money into the project, especially when you need funds to complete the film. Many filmmakers (not only first timers, but the rest of us as well) not only need completion funds, but often start "out of pocket" from the beginning.

Radiance began as a low-budget slide show which I funded "out of pocket." My team and I borrowed images from friends and friends of friends and filled in the holes with pictures from books and magazines. We made dubs of popular and classical music, and bargained for some hard-to-get, unusual special effects as trades. As long as we were creating a draft, and not selling or charging admission for a finished product, we didn't worry about getting permissions. We showed works-in-progress for feedback that included copyrighted material. Later, after making selections from some of the best of what we'd found, we worked on purchasing rights.

I "invested" my entire savings account in this one "calling card." It turned out to be worth the cost and effort. The resulting slide show, *Do Saints Really Glow?* became the centerpiece of our fundraising efforts. One of the lessons I learned from this was how critically important a good trailer or slide show is when it comes to fundraising.

Today, even after thirty years of filmmaking, with a dozen films in active circulation, no matter how much I raise, I almost always end up putting some of my own money into a film during the homestretch. When and if you do that, be careful. You must assume it is a gift to yourself, and that you will probably never get it back.

POINTS TO KEEP IN MIND

To raise money for a film, you must be able to tell your story simply and convey your intention. Speak about the project and your ability to do the job. Underscore the highlights of your track record. Describe past successes in your life and let people know you will succeed. Don't be shy to talk about any awards you've won for other projects. Mention the house parties you've held for the film, the people who have donated thus far, and any shooting you've completed. Get letters of recommendation from individuals who appreciate your work and know your strengths. Include the best of these references with any proposals you submit.

The bottom line is to communicate the strength of your story, your enthusiasm, and your ability to bring the film into being.

An essential element of raising money is building trust. Be very careful not to misrepresent your needs when you are raising money.

The best way to keep from overstating or understating your needs is to give your budget to someone with more experience in filmmaking. Do a reality check. Ask, "Is this budget realistic and accurate?" The closer your budget is to the truth, the better impression you will make.

Your passionate vision, your positive attitude, your trusting relationships — these form the cornerstone of what you need to raise the money for your project.

KEY POINTS

- Every project needs funding in order to come into being.

- The most important piece of the fundraising puzzle is this: People give money to people, not projects.

- Don't limit your fundraising efforts. Everyone you meet is a potential contributor — so keep your mind open and be ready to pitch your project wherever you go!

- Before you begin fundraising, give your budget, proposal, and trailer to an experienced filmmaker and ask for a "reality check."

- When potential donors listen to you, they ask themselves, "Does this person have the drive and integrity to bring this project to the finish line?" Convince them that you do.

- If you plan to seek money from foundations, look at the Foundation Center Online service at *http://fconline.fdncenter.org/*.

- For your first films, I suggest using an existing non-profit "umbrella" organization as a conduit.

- Your attitude is the key to fundraising. Be positive, passionate, and prepared.

CHAPTER 8

YOUR CORE GROUP

1. *Filmmaking thrives as a collaboration.*

2. *A Core Group is a circle of people who support you through the filmmaking process as it goes forward, from vision into form.*

3. *Stay in touch with your core group — by phone, e-mail, or in person.*

4. *One of the great dangers while making your film is becoming overwhelmed by production details and losing track of your vision. Your core group can help you stay focused — and sane.*

Some independent filmmakers spend long months before and even during production, working alone. My experience is that filmmaking thrives as a collaboration, through sharing everything from inspirations to responsibilities. I urge everyone who has the courage to make a film to build a core group of supporters, a circle of people who become your partners and allies, people who believe in you and in what you are doing.

WHAT IS A CORE GROUP?

With every film, there will be people attracted to the project, and to you. Some are old friends, some new. From these people, hopefully, you will find what I call a core group. The phrase "core group" is not a common term in filmmaking. It is a phrase I coined to identify the people who support me throughout production, from inception to completion. I came upon the concept of the core group during the making of my first film. I felt how much difference it made to have another person (my husband in this case) simply listen to me and support me, emotionally, through the ups and downs.

When I embark on a project, I hope to find at least two or three people at the beginning of each film project who will "be there for me" throughout the production.

The function of a core group is three-fold: to keep you aligned with your vision, to keep you flexible, and to support you personally.

If you are running low on funds, your core group might brainstorm with you about how to raise more money. If you are having trouble communicating with someone on your production team, someone from your core group might help you see the situation objectively, and even facilitate working things out.

The quality I look for above all, in addition to mutual caring, is honesty.

A core group member's willingness to tell you the truth, combined with your own ability to listen, will help you survive some of the rough spots of filmmaking. When the relationship works well, it's reciprocal. Your dedication and creativity will inspire the core group members. Their support will enable you. It's a dance. Sometimes you lead and sometimes they do. They may or may not be close with each other. The important connection is their relationship with you.

ATTRACTING A CORE GROUP

Personal Relationships

In the beginning, your core group may consist of just one other person, a family member or friend you respect and trust. I have had core group members from next door, and from thousands of miles away. Right now I have core group members for different projects in Africa, India, and Vietnam.

I know they are there for me; I can feel their companionship across the miles.

When you are drawn toward someone as a potential member of your core group, suggest getting together (if that's possible) to talk about the film and see if there is mutual interest. You may or may not ever use the words "core group." If that person turns out not to be interested in the project, don't let that exchange harm your relationship. If the project is not right for this person at this time (or ever), an honest "Thanks, but no thanks," from someone who is reluctant is a gift. Accept it graciously.

When you include family members or old friends as members of your core group, they may need to adjust their previous impressions to the "new you." These people know you as you have been. Making a film will in many cases turn the filmmaker into a different person — bolder, and more independent. This change might be uncomfortable to people who have known you for a long time. So, be patient, and know there is an adjustment you may both need to go through.

The Larger Community

Sometimes the core group will emerge from the interest group. Our core group for the Ethiopian AIDS films came from among the fifty people who helped transcribe and translate interviews. Among that group were half a dozen people who were willing to give more time. Two had been driving an hour and a half each way, after work, twice a week, to help us.

When we'd translated enough of the footage for the first film so we could begin to assemble the scenes, we needed Amharic speakers (the language of many Ethiopians) to sit with us and make sure that we were editing phrases, cutting between the words correctly.

We decided to hold a weekend retreat to work closely on the editing. We went to Pajaro Dunes, a windswept beach community three hours south of San Francisco. My co-producer, Amy, three Ethiopian volunteers, and I arrived at the house Friday afternoon. We unpacked computers, monitors, transcripts, and set up for editing.

That weekend, the five of us went through every word of every scene in the film — phrase by phrase — to make sure we had each word in the subtitles translated and placed correctly. We barely had time to take a walk on the beach.

We finished late Sunday afternoon and, as Amy and I said goodbye to each of our Amharic-speaking volunteers, it was clear to everyone that we were all solid members of a core team. They remained by our side throughout the production of all five films in the series, and were among the first in line at the theater for the premiere.

By volunteering, they were able to support the creation and distribution of a series of films that were important to them and to their fellow Ethiopians. They were drawn to volunteer because they saw a tragic situation — the scourge of AIDS in Ethiopia — and this was one way to help.

WORKING WITH YOUR CORE GROUP

It's important to stay in contact with the individuals in your core group throughout the project. You don't have to have formal meetings, but you do need to find a way to stay in touch. You may meet in person, by e-mail, or by phone. If you choose to schedule regular meetings, perhaps once a month, people can save the date.

For *Motherhood by Choice* five of us met weekly, then bi-weekly for almost two years.

These meetings should be exciting, a time to share updates and offer suggestions. Remember, these people want to see you succeed because they care about you and share your vision. Whether you get in touch for an emergency or to share a breakthrough, the important thing is to stay in communication.

COMMITMENT

One the greatest dangers you will face in filmmaking is losing track of your vision while getting stuck in the details of production. Members of your core group can often help you get through those situations.

When you begin a film, you are ignited by the spark of an idea. It is critical to stay in touch with this energy throughout the project. As a production goes forward, there are bound to be distractions — people problems, technical problems, and logistical problems — that will dim or seem to snuff out your flame. Equipment breaks, people don't show up when they say they will, or a camera fails just before you start shooting.

When you burn out, the people in your core group can remind you of your original intention.

Honesty

Because you need to tell your core group that you want them to be candid with you, what you hear may be painful.

Sometimes people in your core group will give you input that is embarrassing. They may notice that someone on your production team is not supporting you, and you've been in denial. Or in a feedback session, they may tell you that you've lost track of the central point of the film. These people may be the only people who can tell you these things.

When I was making *Radiance* someone close to the project pointed out that I was "caught" in the light. It would be more effective if there were archetypal images of darkness, to contrast with "the light."

At first, I resisted. I became defensive, and protective of my original vision. After I stepped back from my first reaction, I decided to try a few images of darkness, beginning with an ancient tomb in shadows.

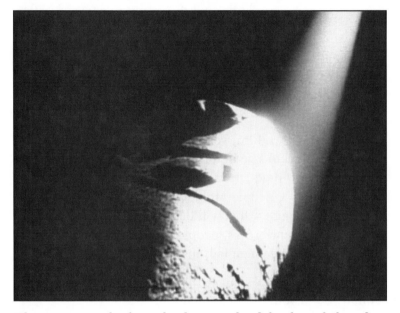

That section, which evolved to speak of death and the after-life, went on to become one of the most provocative scenes of the film. I listened to the critical feedback, resisted it at first, then incorporated it.

Listening

Members of your core group will often be your most candid critics. Here's a simple two-step technique for listening without becoming defensive.

1. Assume that the *other person may be right*.

2. Make it your goal to simply *understand what the other person is saying*. Don't agree or disagree. Instead, just listen.

This doesn't mean that you always have to do what someone in the core group tells you. There are times when you need to ignore input, but remain open to suggestions.

When I was making *Why Do These Kids Love School?* several people close to the project pointed out that I was only filming schools that encouraged academic freedom, and that I was creating a biased film that would have limited distribution. They said I also needed to show traditional schools with stricter programs.

I listened, but what people were telling me didn't feel right. I considered their feedback, and in this case, did not take the advice I was being given.

People urged me to show "the opposite." I knew, intuitively, that showing examples of this creative approach to learning was enough, and was its own story. I stayed with my original vision of letting the images speak for themselves — children moving freely, excited about learning. I didn't need to show them sitting quietly at separate desks by contrast.

Why Do These Kids Love School? went on to become a popular PBS prime time special in 1990. Two days ago I got a bulk order for the new DVD from an activist progressive education group.

Because I followed my intuition, and told the truth about what I felt and observed, the show has enduring qualities that have kept it in active distribution a generation after its first release.

Crisis Support

Telling people up front that you might need them to "be there," occasionally, in a crisis situation, is another step in the process of being honest with them and with yourself. Their presence and input may be critical during an emergency.

I will never forget the day I found out that one of my staff, to whom I had given check-writing privileges (a big mistake), had been quietly writing checks to herself. I needed emotional support (to say the least), and advice. I took a deep breath, and then called for help. A member of my core team was there soon after I called to help me handle this troubling situation. It got resolved (however painfully), and I am grateful that I didn't have to do that alone. And I had to admit I had made a mistake.

When a Crisis Occurs

1. Accept that you are in crisis.
2. Remind yourself that the pressures of filmmaking might lead to crises, and that these crises can be worked through.
3. Call someone or schedule a crisis meeting.
4. When you meet, tell the absolute truth about what is happening.
5. Listen.

You may or may not be contributing to the crisis. It doesn't matter whose fault it is. The point is to come up with solutions. Remember that the core group's honesty, and your ability to listen, will help you survive the crisis and move forward. When you lose perspective, your core group can also provide a reality check. These people in the core group are there to encourage you, as well as to help you chill out, let go, and open your mind.

They will see you at your most confused and irritated, and at your clearest. You need to be able to talk to them freely, confide in them, and share your concerns without feeling that you have to censor what you say.

KEY POINTS

- The purpose of the core group is three-fold: to keep you aligned with your vision; to keep you flexible so you can move forward; and to support you emotionally and in whatever other ways you need help!

- Insist that your core group be honest with you.

- As a filmmaker, one of the greatest dangers you will face is losing track of your vision while getting stuck in the details of production. A core group will help you get through that period.

- Your core "group" may begin with just one person.

- Be sensitive when you include family members or old friends in your core group. They remember you as you have been, and you are going to change and grow as you work on your film!

CHAPTER 9

THE PRODUCTION TEAM

1. *Many first-time filmmakers try to make their own films, doing almost everything themselves.*

2. *Most filmmakers soon realize that there is so much to do, that they need to work with one or more other people.*

3. *The best place to find crewmembers is the local filmmaking community, if one exists.*

4. *When interviewing someone, pay close attention to your intuition. Do you get a good feeling about this person?*

5. *Write a simple letter of agreement for each person on your team. Update it if the situation changes.*

6. *Always be clear about money.*

7. *Deal with problems and disagreements immediately or as soon as possible.*

Many beginning filmmakers shoot their own first films, and may even try to edit them solo. Eventually, however, just about everyone who makes a movie realizes that production works better as a collaboration, even if only with one other person. Whether you ask a friend to help, hire another cameraperson, or accept an intern or volunteer, making a film will include people who want to help in some way. It will be your job, as the Producer and/or Director, to help your team work well together.

Whether scripting, shooting, or editing, filmmaking often requires working under demanding conditions. The relationships you and they develop while making a movie will be among of the most intense in your lives. The logistics of filmmaking, as well as some of the challenges you and your crew might have to face — sharing space, equipment, and decision-making when people are working long hours — will bring up a range of feelings.

Ideally, relationships among your team members are mutually supportive and people are not working at cross-purposes. To sustain this, you will have to head off the inevitable miscommunications and frustrations.

As independent filmmakers, we are well known to become immersed in the work, sometimes to the point of "distraction." We have to be sensitive about making excessive demands on the people working with us. Some of your team will not be as eager as you are to endure the hardships you put yourself through.

When you consider people for the team, keep in mind that not only you, but the whole team might be working side by side for at least a year. The more people on the job, the more personalities there are who will need to get along with each other. Ideally, everyone working with you will be committed to supporting each other, communicating candidly, and working out problems as they arise. However, things are rarely that simple.

Ultimately, it is your job, as the filmmaker who brought them all together, to ensure that everybody on the project feels satisfied, challenged, and appreciated. While this idyllic harmony is not humanly possible to maintain all the time, strive to achieve an atmosphere of goodwill whenever possible.

Bringing Together the Right People

Finding Team Members

The best place to start looking for crewmembers is the local independent filmmaking community, if one exists. This community can be broadly defined, to include film teachers and students, filmmakers, both commercial and independent, as well as people working at the local TV station. You might tap into this community by taking filmmaking classes at local colleges, joining local filmmaking organizations, or volunteering to help local filmmakers on their productions.

Additional ways to find people are on the Internet, through newsletters, and by posting "help wanted" ads on the bulletin boards of local college film departments or cable access stations. If your community doesn't seem to have these facilities, expand your geographic reach. You might find recent film school graduates in nearby communities who will volunteer for the opportunity or a modest hourly wage. There are also experienced production personnel, or those in film-related careers such as still photographers and sound people, who want to work on something non-commercial or sometimes simply want the opportunity to work on a movie. And then, there are those who believe in your subject and want to help *pro bono*.

Although there is no one way to do this search, if you persist, you will eventually find at least a few people. As the project progresses, others who may want to work on your production will hear about your work, and check out the opportunities you offer.

When I started out in Menlo Park thirty years ago, I had few peer companions. I drove to San Francisco for meetings, hired crew and got a few volunteers from San Francisco and Berkeley. I decided to see who else was out there. So I sent a notice inviting a wide variety of people in a radius of about twenty-five miles who might be interested in filmmaking to gather and share interests and skills. I was astonished when fifty people showed up! Everyone else was similarly surprised. Many of us didn't have any idea there was this community so near by. We began to work together, called ourselves IMAGE (Independent Media Artists) and that group continued to meet, one way or another, for more than ten years. So, there is more help out there than you may realize!

How Many People Do You Need?

When you move beyond doing everything yourself and set out to assemble a crew, start with the smallest number you think you need to get the job done.

For me, the smallest practical crew on a shoot is two, myself to direct, help out, and do the interviews (if that is what we are doing), and a cameraperson who also handles the sound. Having the cameraperson do sound is not ideal, but in fact one person handling camera and sound often does a fine job. Many filmmakers feel that a cameraperson will be too involved with shooting images to do a good job managing sound. But on a limited budget, you improvise.

In postproduction, the smallest practical crew for me is also two: an editor and myself. You can add other people in post-production as you need them: an assistant editor, a musician, a bookkeeper, or a research assistant.

There are no strict rules for independent filmmaking, except to feed the crew, and pay them the rate on which you agree.

Sometimes my crews and volunteers have exceeded twenty. But still, I know I can do almost anything with two.

As your budgets and needs expand, so will your crew.

What Do You Look For?

When you evaluate people for a position, consider:

- ☙ How does this person relate to you? To the others on your team?

- ☙ Does this person have the skills? Or, if an intern, is there a genuine interest in learning the skills?

❧ Is there an interest in the subject of the film? Obviously, interest level is more important for someone who is directly involved with production than someone you bring on for one shoot.

Another quality to look for in potential candidates is character. Look for someone who is straightforward. Do you get the sense that this person will do what he or she promises?

When you evaluate someone it's a good idea to talk to other filmmakers who might have information. Check references as well as checking out your hunches.

I once worked on a production with a person about whom I had good feelings initially. Unfortunately, I had not checked any references. As we worked together, supposedly as peers, I began to feel uneasy. I finally decided to talk to people in the business who knew him. When I checked, not a single person had anything good to say. Some reported that he had a long history of exploiting other filmmakers. But I didn't get this information until I asked.

So, do your due diligence. When you contact a former employer or colleague for a reference, ask, "What was your experience working with this person? Do you have any observations you can share?" Generally, people don't tend to offer negative feedback unless you ask in a way that makes it safe for them to be candid. One question to always ask is, "How does this person get along with the rest of the team?"

The Process of Selection

Although your instinctive responses provide a starting place, you also have to evaluate people objectively.

When I bring on a new team member, I often suggest a trial period for both of us. I might take someone on as an intern for a month. I observe how that person deals with different aspects of production, and the intern sees if it feels like a good match as well. With a new shooter or editor, I do the same. Everyone needs to see how it works.

Striking a Balance

When you are interviewing someone who might be on your team, pay attention to your instinctive reactions. Do you have a good feeling or is there something that makes you uncomfortable? Film production is an intimate journey, so choose your traveling companions wisely!

There are times when your needs will supersede those gut reactions. Sometimes you are desperate for someone with a certain skill. Maybe you need to find an affordable shooter immediately.

You hear that X is available and you think, "I don't feel great about X and I've heard from others he doesn't take direction well, but…." At this point you may need to overlook your previous impressions of X.

If you choose this shooter, be respectful and professional. Compromise is at times necessary on any production with a limited budget. You will be weighing intuition and knowledge versus immediate needs and budget — at every stage of production.

WORKING TOGETHER

Managing Expectations

The best way to avoid problems with your crew down the line, is to set realistic goals at the outset.

For example, when you are working with a new editor, make your expectations clear. If you want to sit with the editor for all the fine-cutting decisions, make sure that is understood up front. If you expect your editor to do more — review all the footage, come up with a story line, and suggest the strongest scenes — make sure that what you expect is explicit. Some editors can come up with a story line and see the strongest scenes easily. Others are primarily technicians and don't have that skill. Find out what is going to work best for you both.

A low-key, but still professional way to make sure everyone understands what you expect of each other is to write a simple letter of agreement. When you agree on what you expect of each other, sign and file the letter. It is a good idea to write one of these letters or "deal memos" with every person on the crew. Most filmmakers don't do this, and many wish they had.

Be very clear about money. If any money is changing hands, whether in the form of fees, salary, or royalties — anything — I recommend that you put the details in writing. Then, make sure you and the other person are in agreement on the terms before you start working together.

As people's roles change, update the letter. Someone may do more than expected, or less than originally anticipated. If this happens, consult with the person, revise the letter, and put it back in the files. Reaching these agreements is not difficult if you have good communication with your team.

I try to have regular meetings with my whole team. I usually have a general agenda and each of us reports on our activities. We share information, concerns, and progress about all aspects of the production. These meetings help to maintain a community spirit.

Sharing Responsibilities

If you leave a new editor alone for a week and hope you will get what you want, you are taking a risk. Clarity is the cornerstone of a good production team. Either let the editor know exactly what you want, check in regularly, or sit side by side.

Even if your director/editor relationship is good, you still have to stay in communication.

Similarly, you need to let your videographer know what you want. He or she can shoot without you directing every move, but at the outset of each shoot, you need to state your goals.

When you understand everything that is happening on the production, you can take responsibility for delegated decisions to be made in your name. Ask questions whenever you don't understand what is happening. Ask persistently until you find out what you need to know. Then, when you need to delegate, you will understand how to communicate what you need.

As you develop deeper relationships with your crew, you will be more confident about handing over more responsibility without monitoring every task. The challenge is to delegate while staying aware of what is happening in all phases of production.

Problems and Disagreements

When there are interpersonal conflicts, always try to address problems immediately. They usually can be cleared up with a one-to-one meeting. When left to fester, misunderstandings or disagreements become more difficult to heal. As soon as you sense that something is wrong, arrange to meet privately to discuss the problem. In this meeting, share your concerns with sensitivity and tact, but still be candid. Explain what is true for you, and make it safe for the others to do the same.

YOUR RESPONSIBILITIES

Talking to Your Team

Problems come up during every production. You may be in cash flow crunch, or you may not be able to get the resources that you need. When this happens, the best policy is to tell the crew the truth, if possible. There will always be situations in which you don't need to or want to tell everyone.

For example, if you are running low on money, you should let the crew know, because they count on you for their paycheck. However, you would not need to tell that to volunteers and certainly not interviewees. If a piece of equipment needs to be replaced, and you can't afford a replacement, you need to let anyone who might use that equipment know what is happening. You also may need to tap into your core team for advice on emergency fundraising.

Don't Overwork Your Team

At times, in the past, when we've been on deadline, I have encouraged crew, especially editors, to work exceptionally long hours. I say "in the past" because I learned the hard way not to do that. One of my finest editors, with whom I had a close, trusting relationship, worked long hours because at first she wanted to please me and wanted to earn the extra money. As time went on, she became resentful. She didn't tell me this directly. She confided her frustration to other staff members. A feeling of negativity began to seep into the office.

Finally one of the other staff members confided to me that this editor was criticizing me to others, but never to my face. I had a private meeting with her, long after I should have. She reluctantly expressed her unhappiness, letting me know that I was asking her to work more than forty hours a week, and she wasn't being paid overtime. She was right. I immediately cut back her hours, and offered her overtime pay whenever we went past a forty-hour week. We agreed that she would stay on until the end of the production, but no longer. She had been with me six years. She left with credits for jobs well done, but those last weeks were very painful for us both.

A month after she left, a mutual friend told me that she had become ill while working on the film, with a lingering low-grade infection. If I hadn't been so fiercely intent on finishing the film right then, I might have admitted sooner that something was wrong. If I had admitted to myself she looked sick, I could have asked her to take time off, get some rest, and take care of herself. Or hired a replacement.

The point of this story is that you are responsible for your team and you have a responsibility not to overwork them. Don't go into denial, as I did. And a key to that is good communication on both sides. I hadn't made it safe for her to talk to me and she hadn't confided in me.

As sad as this story sounds, years later we became good friends again. Recently, she wrote me a long, very loving letter, about the richness of our time working together.

AVOIDING PROBLEMS

You Are the Captain

Literally, and figuratively, you are the captain of the ship. Bottom line, you are responsible for everything that happens.

Money

The subject of money brings up another caution related to the crew. Never give a crewmember sole signature authority on a bank account. If you do decide to share signature power, set up the account so checks require a dual signature. That way you will be aware of each expenditure.

Misunderstandings about money will complicate the entire production and, in extreme cases, you can end up in court. Most people don't think that would ever happen. Bottom line: Put everything in writing, know where the money is going, and do not give away the responsibility for handling it.

Decisions

Sometimes you will need to give others responsibility for important decisions about the production. You may need to be away for an extended time, or you may just be short-handed. When you assign any responsibility to someone else, you need to communicate exactly what you want. If you hand off responsibility without being clear, you are asking for trouble.

The principle of communicating expectations would also apply to a large production with a separate production manager or line producer whose job it is to manage the budget. Don't hand off responsibility to anyone without being clear about your expectations, whether it is an intern, editor, or cameraperson.

Suggesting a Trial Period

Ideally, you try to find staff members who work well on a team, and who will share your vision. But it's not always possible to know in advance. Plus, you can't always find or afford the "right" people, and you have to do the best you can. There are also lovely surprises: People who weren't excited when they started can become intrigued and increasingly committed as the project progresses.

Always consider a trial period. This will give you a chance to work with people as they are. You don't need to build them up in your own mind to justify having them on the project, or project onto them your positive hopes for their participation. During a trial period, you can both see how it is working.

If there isn't a match — say for someone who wants an internship in editing — but you like the person, you might say something like, "I know you wanted to edit, but that is not where I need you most right now. But because you have good computer skills, are you willing to begin by committing a few hours a week to working on our database?"

Evaluate your feelings about people, consider their qualifications, listen to what you hear, and make your best guess. There will always be surprises, both ways!

If you don't get a clear "read" on all measures, then the question becomes: Can you table your concerns, and use this person on the project in a limited way or for a limited time?

If you decide to go forward despite some misgivings, begin by being honest with yourself. If it isn't working, deal with the situation as soon as you can.

Letting People Go

At some point, you may have to ask someone to leave even though his or her part in the project is not complete. We all want these relationships to work out. However, not all filmmaking matches are made in heaven.

Your goal for all situations when things are not working well should be to acknowledge your differences in a way that allows other people to continue to work with you and accept your leadership. If that does not work, then be as respectful as possible about parting ways.

It is hard to tell someone there is no longer a place for him or her on the team. You may be tempted to delay that decision because you don't want to hurt someone's feelings. You may delay the discussion for selfish reasons, because you still need that person. Perhaps you can't replace him or her easily.

However, once you've made a decision that someone is not going to work out, have that conversation as soon as possible. Explain your decision and your reasons, and try not to become defensive if the person doesn't agree, thinks you are wrong, and communication becomes difficult. Reaffirm goodwill if that is possible.

If You Lose Control

Even with a good team, and when everyone seems to be getting along well, personnel problems related to control might arise. Sometimes these issues, particularly related to production itself, are not easily solved. A cameraman starts shooting what he wants to film, instead of what you wanted, or an editor begins to turn the a story away from what you had in mind and isn't sensitive to your input. How can you tell whether your vision is being appropriated, or whether people are offering you a gift, however indirectly, and forcing you to look at things that you couldn't see yourself at first? There's sometimes a fine line between respecting the professional expertise of a crewmember and allowing that person to take over a piece of the production. If you don't pay attention and speak up, a crewmember working at odds with you can derail a production.

I once worked with an associate producer who was quietly promising opportunities to some of my volunteers, and using them as his volunteers on weekends without telling me. When I found out, the volunteers were very apologetic. Some stayed, some left, the situation was embarrassing for all of us, and my relationship with that particular associate producer ended civilly and immediately.

Remember that the buck stops with you in every way. The financial buck, the artistic buck, the production buck, the personnel buck. Stay alert, and make it clear at all stages of the process that this is your production.

KEY POINTS

🍂 The relationships you form while making a movie will be among the most intense of your life.

- When you choose someone for your team keep in mind that you all might be "living with" each other for a year or more.

- When you assemble a crew, begin with the smallest number you need to get the job done.

- When you are interviewing a crew or staff prospect, one of the first things to notice is your intuitive reaction.

- Always ask for, and check, references.

- One of the important ways to maintain your leadership is by understanding everything that is happening on the production.

- Be willing to let people go when they are not working out.

- Your relationship with of each of the people on the team has to be both productive, supportive, and above all, honest.

CHAPTER 10

INTERNS AND VOLUNTEERS

1. *Interns and volunteers can help in every phase of production.*

2. *Your passion will attract potential interns and volunteers to the project.*

3. *When you interview potential interns or volunteers, find out what they want to learn and to offer.*

4. *Ask yourself "Is this a good match?" Pay attention to your instinctive reaction.*

5. *Proceed cautiously after taking on an intern or volunteer. Start with small tasks, and see if this person is compatible with the rest of the team.*

Most independent filmmakers can offer opportunities for interns and volunteers in every stage of production. Whether holding a microphone, transcribing interviews, doing research, or setting up screenings, interns and volunteers can be integral members of your team. While working with you, they are able to acquire skills in many aspects of filmmaking.

When I work with interns and volunteers, I am struck by the spirit of generosity that they bring with them. They usually work without pay, and, at the end of their time with the team, they thank us for letting them share in making the production happen.

When you believe in your project, your passion will attract people. Working side by side with you, they feel engaged. In turn their freshness and their enthusiasm will energize the production.

Katie P. had just been accepted into graduate school when she came to a screening of one of my films. After the screening, I answered questions from the audience and discussed the process of making the film. Katie was inspired; she wrote and asked if she could come to work with my company and while there learn as an unpaid intern. After a few weeks of exchanging e-mails, we agreed to a six-month internship.

She postponed graduate school, told her partner she was coming to California, and moved to San Francisco. She interned for a few months, and did so well that I hired her as our administrative assistant at full salary. After running the Concentric office and coordinating productions for two years, she produced a film with us, *Motherhood by Choice*, which has sold over forty thousand DVDs! At the completion of her time with us (three years later), she reapplied to graduate school and has just completed her Master's degree in Urban Planning with a concentration in social and community development. Katie recently reported that many of the skills she learned with us have been invaluable in her new career.

THE DIFFERENCE BETWEEN INTERNS AND VOLUNTEERS

An intern usually has a career goal in mind and wants to learn new skills. A volunteer works with the goal of donating time to help with a specific project.

Interns

An intern usually makes a longer-term commitment, and often works for the duration of a project. Goals for an intern might be:

- To learn a specific skill
- To build a film-related portfolio

- To make contacts in the world of documentary filmmaking

- To support a cause and make a contribution while developing skills

Interns may wear many hats: researching, assisting the editor, supporting the camera people, helping the producer, or handling office tasks (incoming communications, coordinating schedules, shipping, etc.). The relationship you have with an intern usually covers a broader range of activities than with a volunteer.

Volunteers

Volunteers come in and help with tasks, like transcribing interviews or answering the phones for a few hours. In some cases, they might take on far more responsibility, such as doing a research project. Volunteering runs the gamut from a short-term assignment of a few hours to several months, or even more than a year.

The goals that volunteers bring with them vary. Some might be:

- To be of service

- To work with and meet new people

- To participate in an interesting project

- To develop personally

- To explore a new career direction and "test the waters"

CHOOSING INTERNS AND VOLUNTEERS

When interviewing new people, whether staff, interns or volunteers, the first question to ask is, "How will this person fit with the team?" Sometimes the team will spend more time working with interns or volunteers than with you. However, if it seems like a wise choice to you as a team member, you might decide to work with a volunteer on a one-to-one basis.

Interns and volunteers should feel that they are part of the process from the very beginning, and working with you directly might sometimes fill that need. They might not sit in on all of the production meetings or budget discussions, but in as many areas as possible, they should feel "connected" to the project in some way.

"Is This a Good Match?"

The first thing to look for in an intern is genuine enthusiasm, whether for filmmaking in general, or for the subject of your project. I've had interns from many different worlds: social workers, software engineers, a soccer mom, an attorney, a dermatologist, a dance instructor, a primary school teacher, domestic violence counselor, a librarian, and graduate students in everything from sociology to technical writing, plus a wide range of filmmakers.

I always try to find out what interns want before we make an agreement. If I cannot meet their needs, I need to let them know that right away. If a potential intern is interested in some phase of production, I ask if he or she has shot, edited, or produced something. If so, we watch some footage together, and then have a discussion.

I always check to find out how a potential intern feels about the subject of the film on which we are working. My films are about emotionally complex social issues. If someone isn't comfortable with the subject matter, it generally won't be a good match.

When you choose interns or volunteers, you are getting new team members, who are being "paid" in learning and satisfaction instead of money. Tune in to your intuition as you would if you were choosing a crewmember. Trust your instincts, check references, and talk to people in the industry who may know the person.

Compatibility

The issue of compatibility is crucial on a small production team. Even after I accept someone, I still proceed cautiously at first. Generally, we agree to a trial period.

I begin by giving the new intern a small task and see how it goes. If it is not working well, I let the intern finish the task and then we discuss how it might work better. If it continues not to feel like a good match, we usually part on good terms. This way the intern leaves with a small, but complete, experience. When I first started making films, I often "hung in there" even if things weren't working well. I wanted the free labor and the intern wanted the opportunity. I now know (and can admit) that if it is not working, to continue is no favor to either of us.

Working with Interns and Volunteers

It is important to give a new person a guided tour of production and outreach activities, with a chance to look at everything that is going on. This "tour" is part of finding a match between your needs and the intern's interests.

When I accept interns, we enter a teacher/student relationship. I teach by immersion, and the interns learn by osmosis as well as through hands-on experience. I introduce them to a task, such as fulfilling orders, and they learn how to do everything connected to completing that task — from pulling tapes and DVDs, to packaging them, to entering the information into the database.

If, for example, several interns are working on grant writing, they might go to the funding library in San Francisco, read other grants that have been funded, and then write the initial draft of a grant application for one of our projects.

When working with interns, the optimal goal is to dovetail peoples' strengths, matching what they want to learn, and what you need.

One person may be accomplished at Internet research. Another might be drawn to editing, and yet another to camera work. When you give interns freedom to learn and support those efforts, their strengths develop and they find their own best place.

When our intern Kristen was ready for web design, Molly, who had skills and experience, taught her the basics. Kristen had a knack and went on to be our webmaster for a while.

Another recent intern, Katie L., had a feel for editing, so I gave her a stack of interview tapes and said, "See what you can do with these." She put together a riveting assembly cut. We worked together to refine it, and she loved the challenge and is now on staff as a senior editor.

For many interns and volunteers, a satisfying experience is helping to set up and run large feedback screenings. (See Chapter 16 for a description of feedback screenings.) In a way, these work-in-progress showings are like mini-premieres.

Before the screening, interns can publicize the event locally with e-mails and on bulletin boards, organize the room, and prepare handouts. During the screening they can watch audience reactions and give people forms to fill out. After the screening, they can review and analyze feedback forms, and follow up with thank-you notes. Once a new direction is set based on the input, depending on their skills, they might help support editing or re-shooting.

They get to become more involved in the community, meet new people, and learn how feedback from an audience is used to create a powerful film.

Sometimes, I hire an intern as a staff member after the internship is complete, at the outset for a small salary. Most of my current production team began as interns. After an internship, I know who they are and they understand what we do and what our goals are.

What Interns and Volunteers Take Away

It is satisfying to think about what interns and volunteers gain from the experience of working with us.

Interns come away having worked on a product which is tangible, whether it is a successful grant proposal, being part of an edited movie, or their own demo reel. It is important to me that everyone involved with production gets a solid credit on the film, including interns and volunteers.

Ideally, they come away from their time with us with exposure to a filmmaking experience, and a project they can point to later and say, "I was part of that."

KEY POINTS

- Interns and volunteers are integral members of your independent production team.

- Interns and volunteers bring energy, freshness, and a spirit of generosity to the production.

- The task of choosing interns and volunteers is as important as that of choosing staff and crew.

- Interns should take away an experience and sometimes a product for which they feel some ownership.

- Volunteers acquire new contacts, an exposure to filmmaking, and a feeling that they have contributed to a project that will be seen by others.

PREPRODUCTION PLANNING: GETTING READY TO SHOOT

1. *The treatment breakdown becomes the template for pre-production planning.*

2. *Create a production binder early in the process.*

3. *Select initial interviewees (if you are doing interviews).*

4. *Whenever possible, scout locations in advance.*

5. *Use a shot list so you don't get distracted and miss critical shots. You can depart from it any time.*

6. *Always get interviewee releases on — or before — the day of the shoot. It is often extremely difficult to get releases after an interview.*

You may spend one hundred hours preparing for one hour of shooting, and the next day you might have to pull together a shoot in one hour! Both time lines are part of the independent filmmaker's world. Preproduction planning is a way to prepare yourself for both of these eventualities.

In this chapter we will talk about ways to get ready before the shoot to help things go smoothly and minimize problems.

When you go into the field, events will happen that you can't control. Fuses blow. Strangers walk through the frame. Airplanes fly overhead during interviews. Videographers have family emergencies and need to leave on a moment's notice. Every filmmaker faces unforeseen events in the field. After you've made a few films, needing to cope with the unexpected is expected. Meanwhile, the best preparation for those things is to do as much preproduction planning as possible. Then deal with whatever happens!

A Treatment Breakdown

Using your treatment breakdown, you can estimate the number of shooting days, travel costs, and locations. You can decide on the best time to schedule interviews, and make sure you talk to all the interviewees that you need for your film. (See Chapter 7, Crafting the Budget, for a step-by-step description of the treatment breakdown.)

YOUR PRODUCTION BINDER

An efficient way to organize information and keep important facts at your fingertips is to start a three-ring binder at the beginning of your preproduction planning. The production binder will evolve as you add to it over the months. Larger productions will require several binders. The binder should contain:

- Treatment or project description

- Contact information for everyone involved in the production, including crew, interviewees, property owners, suppliers, caterers, nearby hospitals, emergency numbers, doctors, and supporters

- Copies of relevant background research, including maps, pictures, articles, web pages, and bios

- Copies of completed signed permission forms/model releases (keep the originals in a safe place, somewhere else) and several blank model release forms

- Copies of completed location releases (keep the originals in a safe place, somewhere else) and several blank location release forms

Selecting Interviewees

The first step toward selecting strong interviewees (if your film is going to have interviews) is finding people who are interested in the subject and/or whose lives have been touched by events in the story. It is from these people that you will get the most emotionally engaging material. You may have to pre-interview many people before you find the person who has had the right experiences or has engaging stories to tell for your film. Stay true to your vision and look for interviewees who capture the spirit of what you are looking for.

Finding People to Pre-Interview

Begin your search by looking within your own circle of contacts. You probably already know people who are interested in the subject of your film. Among them, you will find leads to the right people to get started. Some filmmakers begin doing audio interviews, an inexpensive and efficient way to get a feel for how someone communicates. Use a good microphone, just in case the interview goes well, and you later decide to use the audio in your film.

At the end of each interview you might ask, "Would you recommend anyone else I should talk to?" Slowly, you will begin to build a network of people who know people, or who know of others. You will often find your best interviewees several steps from where you started, through a network of contacts — someone who knows someone who knows someone.

In your own community, you will probably be able to interview people who know who you are. Access to people in a community where you are not known is more difficult. Before people will agree to interviews, they usually need to feel that they can trust you. You may not have time to build trust with each person you want to interview. This is where getting know a "gatekeeper" comes in.

Try to seek out and befriend a trusted, respected person in the community in which you want to film, someone who can tell others that you are "okay." This connection may come through someone who knows you and knows the person you want to interview. Perhaps it is someone who doesn't know you, but has seen your past work and knows your credentials. Your initial contact with a gatekeeper might come through an e-mail, or a telephone conversation. Sometimes a visit is necessary. When you earn the gatekeeper's trust, that person can vouch for you and will tell others "It's okay to talk to this filmmaker."

Conducting a Pre-Interview

A pre-interview is an exploratory conversation. Once you have identified a potential interviewee — and have gained access through direct contact, gatekeeper or trusted mutual acquaintance — arrange for a telephone conversation, or a brief informal meeting if possible. During the pre-interview, try to find out if this story or what this person is qualified to talk about fits with your documentary. Look for people who are inherently compelling, have interesting stories to tell and to whom you are drawn.

Use a Good Microphone When Pre-Interviewing

If you are able to arrange an audio-only pre-interview, use a good microphone. That way, if someone does tell you a great story, you might still be able to use the sound.

Once you express interest, someone may want to tell you an entire story during a pre-interview. Gently interrupt, and say, "Let's wait until we're together for the actual interview, and then you can tell me the whole story."

That person will only be able to tell you that story "for the first time" once. Wait until the camera is rolling. In a great interview, the person may reveal personal experiences with all the intensity of discovering something for the first time — and you can only respond genuinely for the first time once to that. Stories shared during a pre-interview lose their freshness during the actual interview. Interviewees tend to try and remember what they said earlier so it is no longer spontaneous. You want to give viewers the sense of being present for a live conversation.

Selecting interviewees is one of the most important decisions you will make. Some are part of the story, and you simply accept them. But when I have a choice, I look for certain qualities — a lack of pretension and an on-screen presence. When you meet people in person you can determine if they have these qualities. Not everyone you pre-interview will be suitable for a particular film. If you feel a person won't come across well on-screen, or is not as familiar with the subject as you imagined, then you need to say (in your own words), "Thank you for your time. I learned a great deal from what you have told me. I don't know yet how many interviewees we will be filming, but we are pre-interviewing many people."

Don't shut the door, because you never know what the future holds. But indicate that you will not be using everyone you pre-interview.

Sometimes someone who wasn't right for your film may recommend others who are a better match. They might say, "You have got to talk to so-and-so who knows more about this than I do, or who has another point of view."

Thus, your list of potential interviewees will grow. And from that list, you will make choices.

SCOUTING LOCATIONS

Once you have interviewees selected, you need to decide what else you need to shoot, and where you will film the interviewees. I find that most interviewees prefer to be filmed in their own homes or where they work. However, there are definitely other possibilities.

Location scouting will head off many field production problems. First you need to decide where you will film scenes and activities that happen in places related to your story. Visiting possible locations a few days before you shoot will help you be better prepared.

Once you find a potential location, run through the following list:

1. Check out the lighting conditions: Where is the sun at what time of day? Are there fluorescent or incandescent lights? Where are the windows?

2. Look for visually interesting places and things to shoot. Bring your cameraperson along, if possible. If you can't, make notes so you can describe what you see and what you want during the shoot.

3. Check the power and electrical connections to make sure there is adequate power for any equipment or lights you plan to bring. Make notes about the locations of the breakers, fuses, and power outlets.

4. Listen for background sounds like the hum of a refrigerator, airplanes overhead, traffic noise, a rush of furnace air, or neighborhood barking dogs.

5. Make notes about access, parking, storage space for equipment cases, the location of bathrooms.

6. If you are shooting outdoors, ask your host if you should notify the neighbors.

7. Ask if there are any special cautions for you to observe. A documentary filmmaking crew might be an intrusion. When people agree to be interviewed, they open their world to you. Be sensitive and treat that world with respect.

Interview Settings

What is the impression you want to convey? That decision will determine where you shoot. Filming someone strolling through a park in casual clothes creates a totally different feeling than the image of someone in a tailored suit sitting at a desk.

For some interviews, you will not have a choice. Interviewees schedules are often tight, and you will end up choosing from a few indoor settings. However, if you and the interviewee have flexibility, brainstorm settings together, and include your film team in that conversation if possible. Additional preparation may be called for. If you decide, for example, to go to a place of work, you will need to do much more preproduction planning in terms of additional permissions and schedules.

The bottom line, whatever you plan to do, is to be as prepared as humanly possible!

THE SHOT LIST

Before you arrive on location, it's a good idea to have a list of the shots you hope to get. This list, known as the "shot list," is a way to make sure that you don't overlook an essential image or sequence of images.

When you make a shot list, use your treatment breakdown, and any notes you have from location scouting to make a "wish list." Making a shot list will often reveal holes in your visualization of a scene. You may realize that you will require more shots than you'd planned or you may need a particular type of shot that you hadn't anticipated.

When you finish he first pass at the list, go through it again and prioritize, and if time on location is limited, trim the list down to essentials. Flag the critical shots, the ones that are truly necessary. If you run out of time while shooting, then you might be able to come back and get the shots you still need at the end of the day.

Documents

The business of documentary filmmaking includes making sure that everything related to getting permission to shoot is in order. Some types of releases are required before you go into the field and some you can get later.

Every film and every country requires different releases, depending on the situation. There are, however, two releases that I get every time I shoot: a "model release" or "signed permission form" from each interviewee. This allows me to use the interview both in the film and in publicity. If an interviewee changes his or her mind about being in the film, and you have their release in writing and signed, you are protected. However, if that does happen, you may still decide not to use the interview.

A location release is the other release I always try to get. Whenever you shoot on private property, check to make sure you aren't shooting without proper permission.

The Most Common Releases

The most common releases that filmmakers need:

When you are in the field

1. Model releases
2. Location releases

Later in production

3. Permission to use copyrighted media
4. Permission to use archival footage

This area is complicated, and the laws change. To be safe, get releases from anyone who is recognizable in any scene, whether indoors or out.

Whenever you shoot without a release, and later try to broadcast, sell, or distribute the footage, you may run the risk of legal problems and damages, so err on the side of caution. Here's a partial list of the kinds of situations whose rules you should investigate.

- Private property

- Public property

- Demonstrations

- Commercial signs and signage

- People at meetings and conferences

- Crowds

- Public parks

- Areas, buildings, and locations where photography is restricted or prohibited by anti-terrorism laws

Warning!

In some countries, filming a "sensitive" site — like a jail or military institution — can result in arrest, and imprisonment. To fully understand how serious this issue is, check out Reporters Without Borders (www.rsf.org). Reporters Without Borders tracks cases worldwide of reporters, journalists, and filmmakers who have been arrested, or disappeared.

If you plan to use any copyrighted media like music or archival footage, stills, graphics, and previously shot footage, you will need a release. Some material might be copyright free, but you need to check carefully to confirm that. Find out whether releases will have a fee or be free — or if they are even available — as soon as you consider a selection.

Most broadcasters and distributors will not touch a production that does not have the proper releases. To be safe, talk to an entertainment lawyer before you go into the field. Find out what releases are required for the people, places, and settings you plan to shoot. Don't put yourself in legal jeopardy.

Some filmmakers' organizations, like Film Arts Foundation in San Francisco (*www.filmarts.org*), offer their members a free or affordable consultation with a lawyer well-versed in the needs of filmmaking.

More Documents

Receipts

When you are doing preproduction, start the practice of getting and saving receipts for everything, both cash and credit card purchases. When your credit card statement arrives in the-mail, being able to refer to a stack of receipts will make it much easier to identify project expenses at tax time.

Letters of Agreement

In many cases, documentary filmmakers work on projects without contracts. However, it is wise to clarify your agreements with at least a brief, simply worded document. You should contact a legal advisor before you write any contract. Many filmmakers are absolutely strict about having written agreements and will not work without one.

I usually draft simple contracts with people who work with me on my films. Admittedly, my trust with some of these people is so complete that I don't feel that I need a written contract.

However, on principle, it is prudent to have a written contract or agreement with everyone.

The Real Reason for Contracts

A contract or deal memo is a way to avoid disagreements later. You and the other person know what to expect from each other. Having something in writing is an insurance policy for both of you.

Though preproduction efforts may cost you time and money in the short run, in the long run they will save you time, money, and heartache. It is well worth the investment to think through potential problems before they happen.

KEY POINTS

- The treatment breakdown will serve as the template for preproduction planning.

- Start a production binder at the beginning of the prepro-duction planning process (three-ring binders work well).

- You may need to pre-interview many people before you find the right interviewees for your film.

- Begin your search for interviewees by exploring your own circle of community.

- Seek out a respected "gatekeeper" to create a bridge to the individual or community in which you wish to film.

- Use a good microphone when pre-interviewing.

- Location scouting will prevent many field production problems.

- The four most common releases that filmmakers need are: model; location; permission to use copyrighted media and permission to use archival footage

- Save all receipts.

- Write simple contracts for everyone with whom you work.

CHAPTER 12

FIELD PRODUCTION

1. *Plan before you go into the field, but be flexible once you get there.*

2. *Meet with the crew before the shoot. Who is on your crew?*
   a. *you alone if you are going solo*
   b. *plus a cameraperson, who is also doing sound*
   c. *plus a sound person if you arrange that*
   d. *possibly plus a production assistant (assistant producer and/or an intern or volunteer)*

3. *Use good microphones, properly positioned.*

4. *Get interviewee releases before you leave the interview.*

5. *Talk to your cameraperson and agree on unobtrusive signals to indicate when you want the framing to change.*

Your biggest challenge in the field is to keep your original vision of the film in mind and find ways to communicate this vision to others. You also need to understand the craft of filmmaking well enough to give people specific direction so they can help you reach the goal.

If you've done your preproduction well, when the time comes for you to go into the field with a crew, your shoot should go smoothly (barring natural disasters and other unpredictable events). However, no matter how much planning you do, when you run into "the unexpected" (and you will), be flexible.

I remember directing a shoot in a waiting room of the local free clinic in Nazareth, Ethiopia. The room had been transformed into a theater. Teenaged girls filled the benches, whispering and giggling as they waited for the play to begin. The Anti-AIDS Girls Club had prepared a play about the dangers to young women in this part of Ethiopia: rape, domestic violence, and AIDS.

I wanted to capture the audience's facial expressions during the play so we had to film the audience from the front of the room. At the same time, we wanted to shoot the action of the play from the back of the room.

We had two cameras, but only one cameraman — our second cameraman had flown back to the U.S. that morning to deal with an emergency. We set up a second camera at the back of the room on a stationary tripod to record a continuous wide shot. Henock, my one cameraman, set up his camera in the front, where he could get close-up footage of the audience.

When I checked the wide shot in the monitor from the back of the room, I could see that some of the most important action was not visible in the frame. I called over our van driver, who was sitting on a bench, waiting to drive us back to Addis Ababa, and asked him, with hand signals (he spoke no English), if he would handle the camera and follow the play from the back of the room.

He agreed, and amazingly, though he'd never shot before, we ended up with great second camera footage! We captured the play, the audience's facial expressions, and even some of what was happening backstage.

Sometimes you have to take a chance and "wing it" in the field.

Going into the Field

One of the best films about making a film in the field is *The Man with a Movie Camera*. In it, Dziga Vertov records a day in the life of 1920s Russia. We see the cameraman carry his lightweight camera and tripod everywhere. He shoots from a moving car, a motorcycle, the top of a bridge, from a bucket dangling over a river, and the middle of a busy street.

Released in 1929, the spirit of the film is ageless.

The Man with a Movie Camera (1929), Dziga Vertov.

BEFORE THE SHOOT

You know what you hope to achieve with the interview. The first challenge is successfully communicating your vision to your crew. Here are a few tips that I have found useful.

Meet with the crew before the shoot, if not the day before, then earlier the same day. Explain your objectives and any special requirements of the location.

Review the shot list. Have copies available for everyone. (See Chapter 11 for a description of the shot list.)

Talk to the videographer and communicate the "feel" that you are trying to achieve. (You might be meeting for the first time on the day of the shoot.)

Hand out copies of contact information, including cell numbers, so people know how to get in touch with you and with each other after the shoot.

Go over the day's schedule. If you are not already on location, hand out maps, with directions.

A SMALL-CREW INTERVIEW

The rest of this chapter describes a special kind of shoot, the small-crew interview.

(There are a number of good books that describe filming a range of situations other than interviews — outdoors, in a wide range of locations, and a variety of lighting situations. The book I usually recommend to people is *Directing the Documentary* by Michael Rabiger.)

At the heart of my documentaries are interviews. I find that one the most powerful tools with which to convey passion is a provocative, engaging interview. While not all documentaries use interviews, I want to give you the tools to shoot a successful interview if you decide to do that. What follows is a detailed description, from what I've learned, of how to set up and run a small-crew interview shoot.

THE DAY OF THE SHOOT

Arriving Early

Plan on arriving an hour before the time of the scheduled interview. If you know where you will be doing the interview, proceed to set up. If you have not been there before, walk around now, with your cameraperson, and choose a place that feels right.

Choosing a Good Spot for an Interview

1. If you are shooting with available light, look for a source of indirect natural light, ideally a "north-facing window."

2. Position the interviewee so the light falls on the side of the interviewee's face, creating either a subtle or a dramatic difference on each side of the face.

3. You want a background that is appealing, but not too interesting! For example, a wall of photos or movement in the background may distract the viewer.

4. Listen carefully. Are there background sounds that will interfere with your audio?

5. Don't be shy about asking to "dress the set" by placing things like plants, books, or pictures behind the interviewee.

It usually takes about forty-five minutes to set up the camera, test the sound levels, and position the lights (if you are using them).

Explain to the interviewee that he or she is welcome to stay in the area while you are setting up, but that you won't be ready for another forty-five minutes.

After the camera is set up, take a look at the image in the monitor or viewfinder, and make sure framing has the "feel" you want.

(When I can, I like to visit with the interviewee while the cameraperson or team does the rest of the set-up.) If you don't have a professional sound person helping you, listen to the sound yourself. Use headphones, and check the quality of voices. Be alert for echoes, and extraneous sound. The audio should be clear and intelligible, without distortion, and as free as possible from outside noise. You may need to unplug a refrigerator humming in the background or stop the whir of a fan in a heater.

Invite the interviewee to sit in front of the camera during the final ten minutes of preparation while you adjust the image and check the microphones for placement and sound quality.

Setting Up Microphones

When the interviewee is settled, position and test the microphones you will be using.

Two Factors That Affect Sound Quality

1. The quality of the microphone(s)

2. The placement of the microphone(s)

You have two basic choices of microphones; a shotgun mike positioned near the interviewee, just off screen, or a small lavaliere mike clipped to the interviewee's clothing

The built-in microphone that comes with most camcorders, or an auxiliary microphone positioned above the camera lens are emergency back ups. Both of these options give poor sound, and neither is recommended.

I believe that a good lavaliere mike is the safest way to get good sound. Lavaliere mikes seem to work best when they are placed six and nine inches from the person's mouth.

Try to arrange the lavaliere mike's wire so it is as inconspicuous as possible. If you can, run the wire up under the interviewee's clothing. Make sure that no clothing rubs against the microphone. Once the microphone is in place, put on the headphones and ask the interviewee to move a little so you make sure there isn't a rustling sound.

Coping with Outside Sounds

Simply ask the interviewee to pause if you hear a loud outside sound, like the motor of a bus or the roar of a jet plane as it passes overhead. However, if the interviewee is in the middle of an emotional thought, it's better not to interrupt. Give a signal to pause when the thought is complete.

The Release

Some directors ask the interviewee to sign the release before the interview starts, some wait until after the interview. Either way, be sure to get a release before you leave. If you don't get a signed release before you leave, you can send it in the mail. For some reason, people are less willing to sign releases after an interview. The rule seems to be, no matter how inconvenient it might be to get the release on the day of the shoot, it will be harder tomorrow.

SHOOTING INTERVIEWS

During an interview, there will be times when you want the cameraperson to reframe the image. Before the interview, go over signals telling your cameraperson when to reframe. Agree on a simple set of unobtrusive ways to communicate when to move in closer or pull back.

You will know, intuitively, what framing is best because you hold a vision for the entire film. A skilled, sensitive cameraperson may know when to get close for maximum emotional impact, but only you know if that shot is what you want at that moment.

Options for Framing

Agree in advance with your cameraperson about general framing and reframing options. A few suggestions:

Reframe only between questions or during long pauses.

Generally, do not zoom in and out while filming. Except in the hands of an extremely skilled cameraperson, zooms and pull backs during an interview are distracting.

Agree on two inconspicuous signals: one to tell the cameraperson when to get a closer shot, and one to pull back and create a wider shot.

Most of the framing during interviews will be a combination of three shots: wide, medium, and close-up.

W (Wide Shot): The wide shot shows the interviewee and the location. This shot gives the audience a sense of the place and establishes the physical details of the place in the mind's eye. Entry-level filmmakers often neglect to get a wide shot. Without a wide shot, you many find it difficult to edit the interview.

MS (Medium Shot): The MS is approximately what the audience would see if they were having a conversation with the interviewee. The face and upper body is clearly visible. This is particularly nice if the interviewee is using his or her hands. When an interview is shot completely in medium shot (without close-ups), the audience may feel remote from, and uninvolved with, the interviewee.

CU (Close-up): The face fills the whole frame in the CU. This framing is usually saved for emotional moments. For some reason entry-level filmmakers often have difficulty shooting close-ups. Don't be shy about shooting close-ups during emotional moments. When editing, close-ups invite the audience to become emotionally involved with the interviewee. When you edit the interview, a few wisely chosen close-ups may give your interview emotional power.

The rule of thirds says that the main points of interest in a shot should fall either one-third or two-thirds of the way up the screen. The eyes of the interviewee should generally fall upon the line bisecting the upper two-thirds of the screen, if possible.

I prefer to have the interviewee looking about five degrees off center. When a person looks directly into the camera, it feels intrusive to the viewer. If the interviewee looks farther away — say twenty degrees or more off center — it is more difficult for the audience to "read" the interviewee's emotions.

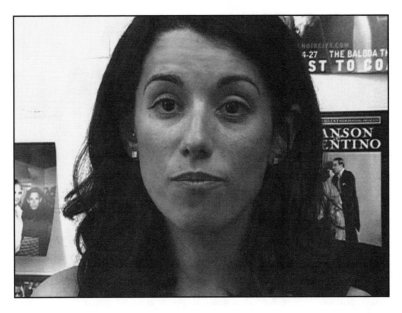

Two Thirds Rule: Eyes properly positioned in the upper 1/3 of frame.

Looking into camera.

Looking five degrees to the side.

Looking forty-five degrees to side.

Lighting

I mostly use available (natural) light. Often, my only lighting source is the light that comes through a window, or whatever other light is available — indoors or out. My approach is to simply experiment with what's available until I get an image that looks good. However, there are many situations which will require lighting, bounce screens, shades, etc.

Lighting for video is a huge subject — and one that we cannot do justice to in this book. The subjects of three-point lighting, back lighting, and lighting for drama occupy entire books in themselves. Another complication is that lighting for video is different than lighting for film.

My own rule for lighting video is close to what veteran cinematographer Paul Wheeler says in his book *Digital Cinematography*, "If it looks right, it is right."

If you are interested in learning more about lighting, I recommend these two books as a starting point:

> *Lighting for Digital Video and Television* by John Jackman
>
> *Matters of Light and Depth* by Ross Lowell

Field Monitor

Whenever possible, have a field monitor available to check lighting and framing. The small flip-out screen on the average camcorder is *not usually* sufficient to give you an accurate color reading.

The best representation of the image you are recording will be one that you see on a properly calibrated field monitor.

If you cannot take a field monitor into the field with you because of logistics or cost, try to spend some time setting up the camcorder for best picture quality— using a good monitor — before you go into the field.

After adjusting the camcorder for optimal picture quality, adjust the camcorder's flip out display to match the image on the monitor as closely as possible.

B-Roll for an Interview

While on location, remember to shoot B-roll and cutaways. B-roll footage shows the events, situations, people, or things that are part of the interviewee's world, and/or what the interviewee is describing. For example: a street scene in the city where you are filming, or an establishing shot of the building where the interview is taking place.

Cutaways show intimate details of the environment. For example: the interviewee's hands, a coffee cup, a cat curled in the sunlight sleeping, or perhaps the view out a window.

You will use the B-roll and cutaways when you edit the interview. The next time you watch a documentary in which people are being interviewed, count the number of seconds a talking head is onscreen. Ten seconds of "talking head" is usually the maximum most viewers want to see of one person talking on screen. B-roll footage of scenes or stills and cutaways visually "cover" the "talking head" after ten seconds or less, or are used to cover a cut in the interview footage.

The exception to this rule is an interview with a famous person or an extremely compelling interviewee. The audience may sit spellbound through an entire hour of "talking head" if the interviewee is a movie star or simply riveting.

A useful rule of thumb is to shoot an additional twenty minutes of B-roll and cutaway footage for every sixty minutes of interview footage.

Wrap Up

At the end of the interview, thank the interviewee for giving you their time and attention. It's polite to check and ask if there are any questions. Be systematic about packing. It is easy to leave things behind when you are preoccupied.

Check the site and make sure you have put things back and are leaving the space as you found it. Plug back in anything you unplugged. Make sure you have the release forms signed.

After the Shoot

It's a good idea to debrief with the crew after a shoot. If you can work it out, plan on taking time to stop for coffee or something to eat. The crew usually has good feedback and may suggest changes for the next shoot. Listen to what they have to say, but defer any decisions until you review the footage. The footage is the real test of what worked and what didn't work.

If possible, try to review that day's footage the same evening. Because you will be tired, there's always the temptation to skip this step. But, if you don't keep up with reviewing the footage as soon as possible after a shoot, soon you will have a backlog. If possible, review the footage on a field monitor. If you don't have one, use a television set. In a pinch, use the LCD screen on the camera.

Take plenty of notes as you review the footage, and don't forget to make notes about sound. If you catch a sound problem that evening, you may be able to correct it the next day.

If you review the footage and find out that you need to re-shoot, don't panic. Rarely will you need to or want to re-shoot an interview. But if you decide to do so, explain why with your crew. After talking to your them, talk to the interviewee. Most interviewees are reasonable, and will respond well.

Hopefully, there were no problems and you are ready to move forward, incorporate what you've learned, and make plans for the next shoot.

KEY POINTS

- Your biggest challenge in the field is to maintain your vision for the film.

- No matter how much planning you do, things you cannot anticipate will arise.

- Meet with the crew before the shoot.

- Plan on arriving on location at least an hour before the scheduled time.

- Check the sound before you shoot.

- Don't leave without the release.

- Agree in advance with your cameraperson about framing and reframing options.

- Shoot at least twenty minutes of B-roll and cutaways for every hour of interview footage.

- Debrief with the crew after the shoot.

- Review the footage each night, if possible.

- For additional guidance — in filming a variety of situations — refer to *Directing the Documentary* by Michael Rabiger.

CHAPTER 13

INTERVIEWS: GATHERING PEOPLE'S STORIES

1. *A good interview feels like an intimate conversation.*

2. *During an interview, follow the interests and emotional direction of the interviewee.*

3. *Your job is to make it safe for your interviewees to share their wisdom and experience.*

4. *If the interview process is handled well, almost every interviewee will give you at least one or two great moments.*

5. *The interviewee's comfort with you will create a sense of immediacy that will reach viewers.*

A good interview will feel to the viewer like an intimate conversation. Viewers can "tune in" and connect with the person who is speaking. Some documentaries don't use interviews, but for those that do, the heart of the story is often revealed through a series of interviews that fit together like pieces of a puzzle

While I'm conducting an interview, I look for the sparks that illuminate what someone is saying. Whether the person is ecstatic or furious, sad or contemplative — these vivid moments filled with feeling are the kernels around which you can build a scene, or sometimes even a whole film.

Throughout every interview you film, observe — and follow — the interviewee's interest level. When an interviewee is genuinely engaged, continue in that direction. Your job is to be an attentive listener, as well as a good questioner.

Sometimes you can hear the tremble of excitement or fear in someone's voice or see a twinkle in someone's eye. That energy — of aliveness — is what will capture a viewer's attention.

For years, I have been taking small appliances to a small repair shop in my neighborhood: toasters, lamps, blenders, whatever needs fixing. One day, when I was talking to the owner, I saw his eyes light up, as he described what he does. That moment set into motion my desire to make *Fixit Shops: An Endangered Species*, a short film about environmental awareness. The subject takes on new dimensions as these repairmen talk about their work. While one of the men repairs a vacuum cleaner, he describes how satisfying it is to make a broken appliance "live again."

As he talks, his hands carefully tease the front panel away from the body of a small vacuum. He delicately maneuvers the screwdriver into a tiny crevice, as he explains how he pays attention to each step in repairing an appliance. He talks about how the shop is part of the community. Interviewing this veteran repairman — as with many artists, craftspeople and others — was best done while he was working.

With his hands busy using the tools of his trade, he'd look up, glance at me, and go back to work. He was comfortable and spoke easily. And best of all, both his voice and his eyes conveyed his love of what he does.

Not All Documentaries Include Interviews

Albert Maysles and his brother David made one of the best documentary films ever — *Salesman*. Instead of interviews, the camera captures people talking about their lives, dreams, and problems as they go through their daily life. When Albert and his brother David film, they seek to be "witnesses to life."

Albert and David Maysles developed a documentary style called "Direct Cinema," in which the filmmaker watches and records.

Salesman (1969), Albert Maysles, David Maysles, and Charlotte Zwerin.

INTERVIEWING

Good interviews are the result of the interaction between you and the interviewee. When you give someone your full attention, and the interviewee feels that you care, ideas are shared in that special moment, that may never have been communicated before.

People sometimes ask, "Are there special techniques for getting a good interview?" The unspoken assumption in that question is that the interviewer somehow controls an interview. The answer is: Make sure all of your interviewees feel valued and safe.

Once reassured that what they say matters, they will usually take the lead. You want them to feel that this interview is an opportunity for them to speak openly, where they can share intimate insights and memories. In one of my films, an abortion clinic doctor says, "When I put on my bulletproof vest this morning, my daughter said to me, 'Daddy, I hope no one kills you today.'" He then adds, "That's what makes it real for me."

If you are an attentive, non-judgmental listener, interviewees will give you these "close to the bone" moments in which you can hear, see, and feel what is most important for that person.

Preparing for the Interview

The actual interview process begins before you meet for the filming. Ideally, you will be able to do some background research on your interviewee's interests and perhaps accomplishments. You might talk to the interviewee, as well as with others and/or do research on the Internet. If you are speaking with an expert, you should know the basic facts about that person's publications and related work in the field. As soon as you feel you have learned enough, stop. Too much information can stifle the chances for discovery. While you need to be informed, you also want that person to be able to surprise you.

Before the interview, prepare a list of questions. You may not use all (or even any) of them, but writing out questions will clarify your intention, and function as a springboard.

Preparing the Interviewee

Before the interview, it is helpful to either call or visit with the person. Things to discuss include:.

- An overview of the project and the film
- How long the filming session will be

☙ Names or subjects that hopefully will be discussed and those that shouldn't be mentioned

For clothing suggest solid, muted colors and fabrics without patterns. Grey, beige, any pale colors are all fine. Strong primary colors like red might glare, bright white sometimes flares. Herringbone and stripes might cause a wavy, rippled, moire effect

Explain that you would like the interviewee to sign a release.

Building Trust

Building trust is the first step. In a trusting atmosphere, the interviewee will share more freely. In your first conversations, be candid with the interviewee about why you are making this film and what your vision is.

There's an unstated question running through this whole discussion of interviewing, and the question is this: How do you establish intimacy? How do you make it safe for this person to be honest? I've found that the best way to begin to establish intimacy is to simply be open, yourself.

When you yourself are open, your way of being helps interviewees overcome their own caution about speaking candidly.

A natural way to create a bridge during the interview is simply to invite people to tell their story. Instead of asking one question after another, give them the opportunity to go deeper, to gradually share intimate details about one subject that interests them.

While you are interviewing people, pay attention to nuance. Listen to the inflections of a person's voice, and stay with their pacing. If you are not sensitive to their rhythm, you will lose that elusive "connection." If they pause, you pause. Allow them to come towards you at their own pace, instead of reaching out toward them too soon. Above all, try not to judge anything you hear when you are talking to people. If they sense that you are judging, rather than just listening, the flow will stop.

If you have a tendency to be judgmental, how can you stop that? Tell yourself to listen and take in the information, but not label it. You really never know in advance, what jewels may come out of an interview. There will be plenty of time later, in the editing room, to evaluate every word.

Even with all this advice, I have to add that there are no magic formulas. What works for you will be as individual and unique as your personality.

Guiding the Interview

Guiding the interview means, first of all, keeping what is said germane to the subject. This means listening for relevant points. Gently bring interviewees back on topic when they begin to drift off or repeat themselves. Some repetition is natural, but if it begins to feel boring to you, say something like, "Let's put that aside for the moment, and go back to (name the subject)." People are usually fine with being reminded to come back on track. If you begin with a few prepared questions, the interviewee will usually let you know where the interview should go.

What "guiding an interview" really means is listening to and responding to the interviewee while helping them to stay focused.

Interviewing Experts

For many documentaries, it makes sense to interview specialists. But be aware that while most experts are well informed, it may be difficult to get "fresh" material. Some have been interviewed too often, some are beholden to the "company line," and cannot risk giving you those candid moments that work so well. Interviewees who have a position within a bureaucratic system tend to tread carefully.

I once interviewed a school superintendent for two hours to get one line, which acknowledged the value of the progressive approaches to learning being used successfully within his school system. Finally, in one sentence, he admitted that he had observed exceptional progress in a certain alternative school.

Sometimes, after you turn the camera off, even an "expert" who has been careful for a full hour not to stray from safe material, may suddenly offer a personal insight. That's when you say, "Do you mind if I turn the camera back on?" If you ask that question in an easy, offhand way, the answer might be, "Okay, I just wanted to tell you this one story…".

Most of my videographers know to keep the camera rolling to be ready when those moments come. When you are first working with a cameraperson, suggest that they not turn off the camera when the more formal part of the interview is complete.

THE SPIRIT OF AN INTERVIEW

The Spark of Truth

When you sense intensity building, give the interviewee feedback to continue. For example, if someone describes a difficult encounter, you might say, "That must have been really hard. Please, tell me more." Let the conversation build. Avoid a back and forth between questioner and someone answering questions.

Don't worry about "getting a good interview." The best interviews happen when the interviewer is receptive, attentive, and actively listening.

Recognizing and capturing the truth of a moment are keys to unlocking the most potent energies of a subject. Recently, I was interviewing an elected representative whose vote had flipped from one candidate to another on a touch-screen voting machine.

He had confided this privately to a close friend, and the friend told me about it.

I called the representative for an interview, and had to debate letting him know that I knew. When I did tell him I knew, he was relieved and eager to talk.

He said to me (nearly a year after it had happened), "Thank you! I have been wanting to talk about this since Election Day."

Once in a while, a question may be embarrassing for you to ask, but it seems important enough to ask it anyway.

Molly, the principal interviewee in *Moment by Moment*, was partially paralyzed from the neck down. During the interview, she spontaneously began to tell us about her feelings of sexuality since the accident. Her candor gave us courage.

My Assistant Producer and I glanced at each other, both curious, and knew what the next question might be. I asked, as matter of factly as I could, if she experienced orgasms.

I prefaced the question by saying, "This question is hard for me, and you don't have to answer if you don't want to."

Her answer was riveting and detailed! A vivid description of her intimate "inner erotic energies" fascinates viewers whenever the film is shown — especially viewers with similar challenges.

Occasionally, without any suggestion from you, an interviewee will move into an area that is not comfortable for you, personally. If you are not at ease, the interviewee may feel your reaction, and need to be reassured that it is okay to continue. You might say something like, "That's a powerful story… please, go on."

It's generally not a good idea to tell your own story in return. You can simply say, "I think I know what you mean," or "I understand."

There's a temptation to get involved with your personal story. You have to differentiate between being open about the project, and revealing personal details. If you are tempted, remember that the interview is not about you. Your full attention should always stay with the interviewee's story and/or information.

The Importance of Integrity

Appearing in a documentary — which might include telling personal stories to untold numbers of viewers — involves a genuine risk.

People might not realize, during the interview, that what they are saying could cause them embarrassment, or potentially damage relationships with family members and others. During an interview, when people are in the flow of what they are sharing, they may be less guarded than usual.

When someone agrees to appear in your documentary, it is your responsibility to act with integrity and responsibility. It means treating people's confidences with respect. It may mean leaving out sections that you yourself realize are too candid. Sometimes, if the interviewee asks you to edit certain sentences out later, then in my opinion you must do that.

Ideally, every person in your film feels good about participating. Interviewees are investing their time and their reputations. The big brother in a family of three AIDS orphans, who'd lost both parents, changed his mind about being in the film *Whose Children Are They Now?* after it was already edited. This was after he had signed the permission form. First he said he wanted to be cut out. He then said, we could use his footage for a cash payment (thousands of dollars).

Although I liked his interview very much, I could not do that. So we edited his interview and beautiful footage of his sisters out of the film. Whether it was that he really didn't want to be in the film or that he was blackmailing me, after that exchange, keeping him in didn't feel right. I had a signed permission form, but I ignored it.

You need to respect not only the interviewees, but also yourself. Taking a stance that protects you requires a complex balance of professional integrity and honesty. Your recognition of what is best for everyone in the long run, requires objectivity. You need to consider your crew, your backers, yourself — all this will become clearer as you continue to work.

For me, keeping that interview in, whether I was legally entitled to it or paid for it, did not have integrity.

At first, in an effort to do the "right thing," you might feel like you are making mistakes, being too harsh with others or yourself. Eventually, you learn to feel the difference between what will make the most exciting film, what seems right by society's standards and what is actually true for you. Integrity is the bottom line, it is your truth in action. Everyone you work with, everyone you interview, and everyone who contributes money to the project will recognize your integrity. I am still learning.

Trust Your Instincts

When an interview takes off in a direction you never anticipated, allow it to unfold, at least for a while. Trust your instincts. You may be tempted, as I mentioned earlier, to remind the interviewee to come back to the topic or to answer a new question. Or, alternatively, consider that the interviewee is opening a new door for *you*, and inviting you to go beyond what you've planned.

You can choose. You might set your questions aside, and respond to what's happening. Or, a combination of both: You might decide to take the lead and invite your interviewee to say more about things that are beginning to arise spontaneously. What you want to discover in every interview is what is most meaningful for the person you are interviewing.

There is no "right way" to do this. Your ongoing challenge is to recognize what is working and what feels right to you.

IF THE INTERVIEW IS NOT WORKING

Sometimes, despite all your efforts, an interview does not flow smoothly. Perhaps the interviewee did not really want to be in the film, but couldn't say "no" to the invitation. Or the questions you've asked do not evoke any meaningful responses. Or there may be a lack of trust, so that the interviewee cannot be candid.

When an interview is not going well, you will know. You may notice that someone is withholding information, or an interviewee's body language is stiff, or you may see a passive slouch that says, "I have checked out."

Pay attention!

This non-verbal information comes through onscreen, and the audience will feel it. These interviews are rarely useful, unless the interviewee's attitude supports a point you are making.

What to Do When an Interview Is Not Working

You have several options:

1. Wrap it up tactfully. Perhaps offer to try again another day. You might be the problem; you many need to do more background work before you meet again.

2. You might offer to redirect the interview and say, "I have the feeling that you aren't comfortable with the way this is going. Are there things you would rather talk about that I haven't asked you? Or, are there things you would rather not talk about?"

3. You can keep going and ignore the discomfort. However, what usually happens is one or both of you become increasingly tense and the interview fails.

If the interview ends sooner than you'd planned because it's not working well, make sure you are supportive and express your appreciation.

Whether the interview didn't work well or goes on for an extra half-hour because there is so much to say, the interviewee should end up feeling respected and acknowledged.

At the end of any interview, ask, "Is there anything else you'd like to talk about?" After a pause, the interviewee might come up with something deeply personal that surprises you completely. Be open to these moments, and give them time to unfold.

After the Interview

Take the time to write a thank-you note to the interviewee. Sometimes people need reassurance after an interview. A person may be thinking, "I can't believe I told that story on camera!" Or "I wish I had said this or that." Your thank-you note will be a kind of closure, let the interviewee know you appreciated their time, and that you intend to treat their confidences with respect.

KEY POINTS

- In documentaries that use interviewees, people's personal experiences often reveal the heart of the story.

- The best interviews feel like conversations, which evolve out of mutual trust.

- You can greatly facilitate a good interview with trust building and interviewing skills, but you cannot "force the river." The best interviews flow naturally.

- Great interviews can happen when you make it safe for people to tell their own stories.

- People will be able to tell you their strongest story "for the first time," only once. Ask interviewees to wait until you are filming to hear the whole story.

- If appropriate, do thorough background research, especially for an interview with an expert.

- Guide the interview, but do not try to control it. Be flexible in order to follow interesting, fruitful tangents in the flow of conversation.

- Watch the interviewee's interest level during the interview. Give the interviewee feedback and encouragement.

- If the interview is not working, acknowledge that and work out a solution, which may be to suggest ending it early.

CHAPTER 14

BUILDING THE STORY

1. *First of all, your film has to be interesting. If it isn't interesting, most people who start to watch it won't finish, and people who finish it, won't recommend it. The best way to make it interesting is to have an engaging story.*

2. *The construction project part of building a story starts in preproduction, continues during editing, and gets shaped in feedback screenings.*

3. *The fine art of building a story is a process of using your intuition to find a way to convey the heart of the story to the viewer.*

4. *As you build the story, continually ask yourself, "How can I keep the viewer's interest?"*

This chapter is about assembling the elements of a story in a way that captures a viewer's interest and creates an impression that lasts beyond the experience of the first viewing.

Building a story requires different kinds of skills: the ability to gather pieces that will intrigue the viewer, and the focused patience to edit the pieces together so that the story works.

The story not only has to be interesting, but it also has to have an inner logic. Each part has to have its inherent purpose and all the parts have to fit together so that that it works as a unit.

The construction project begins in preproduction when you write a proposal, and grows as you identify the potential dramatic structure. Building the story continues in editing as you craft the key moments that you discover in the footage.

Assembling and reassembling continues through feedback screenings, when you put together the most compelling scenes into a rough sequence and show it to others. Viewers may agree or disagree that a certain scene doesn't work. Some may feel that certain information is missing, others that there is too much information. Based on the feedback you get, you go back to the editing room and make changes. You add one character, and take another out. You make a paper timeline and realize that the pacing of the story needs tweaking. You adjust the order of the scenes. The process is a constant back-and-forth between and blending of the intellectual integrity of logic on the one hand, and feeling tone on the other.

As you follow your intuition about what goes where, and what the relationships and timing should be, you work to craft a story that draws the viewer in. Listen with your inner ears to the rhythm of the sequences. Too much narration, or not enough... too short a pause or should those bites be tighter? That's where building a story is a fine art. If you tune in the inner rhythm of your story, and your characters, you will make a film that evolves throughout production and when complete, carries the spark of your original vision.

When we were editing the Molly Hale story *Moment by Moment*, we had a particularly difficult time figuring out where to place the "sex scene."

Molly wanted to be sexual with Jeramy two weeks after her accident, when she was still basically paralyzed from the shoulders down. In real time, this "scene" came toward the beginning of their story. Dramatically, however, it was too early in the story line. So we did a quick assemble edit and moved the scene near the end, which turned out to be too late! We kept moving the scene around, and finally we found a place where it "felt" perfect and ended up putting the scene two-thirds of the way through, at a point when the viewer is ready for a surprisingly fresh, intimate perspective.

Molly has become a fully developed character by then, but there still was a need for certain elements of her healing to be introduced. Now the "sex scene" feels integral to the story, instead of squeezed in.

By using a storyboard and a series of assemble edits, we were able to move the scene around (the construction part), then step back and see it in perspective, until we worked out a way for it to feel right with the flow (the art part). (See Chapter 15 for a description of an assemble edit.)

Choosing a Structure

My way of working could be called "organic," rather than linear. For some filmmakers, the story line has to have a beginning, middle, and end from the first day, even if there isn't a script.

I'll take you through the way I do it, in the hope that my process might inspire you. At least, it will help you consider possibilities as you develop your own style.

When I work on a film, the structure and the storyboard change constantly. The whole process of developing the story goes back and forth between shooting, editing, feedback screenings, and more editing.

The Classic Three-Act Dramatic Structure

As you arrange and rearrange characters, ideas, and events, it's useful to look at your material from the viewpoint of the classic three-act dramatic structure.

Act One. The audience is introduced to the protagonist and the central problem of the film.

Act Two. Adversaries challenge the protagonist and everything he or she stands for and values. By the end of Act Two, it may look as if the adversaries might win. The protagonist is nearly overwhelmed.

Act Three. The protagonist struggles through and resolves the central problem.

While building the story for *When Abortion Was Illegal*, about the "back-alley" days, I began by considering several different ways to structure the film based on my way of telling the story, which is through interviewees.

CHRONOLOGICAL. I could follow the issue by years from the mid-1800s through the turn of the century to the present. A chronological structure would have required extensive historical research, and costly archival footage. I had neither the time nor the money for those.

SINGLE CHARACTER. At first, I planned to focus on one of my great interviewees, Lana, as the "lead character" and use other interviews to complement her story. But I had to weigh other variables. A single-character structure would have required shooting much more footage of Lana. When done in-depth, the single-character approach might have required months of shooting to get the footage needed to build a compelling story of one woman's journey. But more than that, I realized that Lana's story alone wouldn't include enough dimensions. The tragedies of the back alleys involved the suffering of many women.

ENSEMBLE. Let more than one character "tell" the story. This was my choice. I selected three very different women, each of whom would tell different aspects of her own story. The ensemble structure explores multiple stories in some depth, plus brief interviews with another ten people who are parts of the larger story. It also draws many more interviewees to the film, because each character represents a different piece of the story.

After screenings, people ask, "Where did you get all those interviewees?" The answer is "By word of mouth, by patient, persistent phone calls, follow-up e-mails, and many cups of tea."

THE FINE ART OF BUILDING A STORY

Creating a compelling narrative begins with your vision, supported by your skill, your knowledge, and good material. The best storytellers use a combination of intuition, hunches about how to fit together what they've got to work with: the characters, what happens with the characters, and where the action happens.

Narration may or may not be needed to weave the story together. Generally, audiences relate to the story through its characters. I have learned that if my characters are compelling and sympathetic, the film will hold the audience's attention, and people will be drawn in without the need for narration.

Changes

Sometimes, even with a well laid-out structure, the story changes midstream.

When I set out to shoot *Woman by Woman* (in India), I planned to focus on a rare phenomenon, couples working together in communities where women usually work separately from their husbands.

The couples I planned to film were men and a women working side-by-side in villages where other men and women have worked, and still work, with their own sex only for centuries.

Soon after I started pre-interviewing, Sarita, one of the wives, captured my attention. She is a woman in her middle twenties, who works with her husband, who is a part-time rural medical practitioner.

I interviewed her at her home. She sat on the bed, next to the room's single window. Her face was lit from one side by the fading sunlight.

Her eyes pierced the shadows. She looked directly at me, poised, eager to begin. The translator lowered his voice to follow her intimate story about living in a society where women exist in the shadows of their husbands. She spoke of breaking with tradition and stepping forward to speak out about women's rights. Her interview became a centerpiece of *Woman by Woman*.

Before I met Sarita, the film was to be about couples. After our meeting, I was drawn to focus on women, like Sarita, who hold a key to India's future. The core premise of "women stepping forward" which I found within her interview, became the core of the film. And so my plan, to make a film about couples, changed.

There is no one way to "get it right," you just have to feel what works for each film as you put it together.

Once the characters are identified, and somewhat fleshed out, they provide the spine of the story. With a character-driven documentary, keep in mind that the audience will only be able to follow a few main characters. If you have more than one or two characters, you need a strong theme — visual or metaphorical — to carry the family of characters. The theme connecting all the characters will serve as a character in its own right.

As you work with the material, and get to know the purpose of the main character(s), you will sense how many people you need in order to illustrate different points. While making the first film in a series documenting the stigma of AIDS in Ethiopia, we interviewed many who were infected with the virus. Then we had to decide how many people would work as a spectrum of "characters."

We ended up choosing seven, a number which showed the breadth of the epidemic, but still conveyed intimacy as the audience got to know each one. Our basis for choosing the seven was both how candid each was in telling his or her personal story and, at the same time, what new perspective each added. Other minor characters entered throughout the film to help create an overview.

Sometimes the Main Character Is the Filmmaker

In *Sherman's March*, filmmaker Ross McElwee speaks directly to the camera about women in his life and about his relationships as he sets out to follow the path of General Sherman's "march to the sea" during the Civil War.

As he travels across Georgia, he films everyone he meets: interesting women, advice-giving family members, puzzled friends, and the cheerful mechanic who fixes his car. The end result is a gentle and charming picture of McElwee, his encounters, and day-to-day life in the South.

Sherman's March (1986), Ross McElwee.

Developing a Character

As characters move through the story, your job is to show their growth. If a character does not develop, viewers tend to get frustrated, because they're not engaged. As you lay the story out, look for the events and moments that mark the characters' breakthroughs. Pace these moments, so there is a natural progression.

In *Woman by Woman*, we begin with images and chilling statistics of a downtrodden female population — bride burnings, deaths of female infants, women throwing themselves on their husbands' funeral pyres — then on to the stories of three women, each of whom is learning to value herself, and to be of service in her village. Finally, one by one, each breaks with tradition and speaks out.

Character Time

A character's development is related to both time and timing. Character time is the total number of minutes the character is on screen; character timing is the frequency with which we see the character.

Characters need enough time on screen for the audience to discover who the character is and to watch the character develop.

As you listen for the natural rhythm of the story, you will get a sense of how long each character should be on screen. As you watch your rough cuts, you will see that some characters only need to be visible for a few seconds each time they appear. Other characters need and should get much more screen time.

Character Timing

A character may need to appear on screen with increasing frequency as you build to the climax of that individual's story. You will get an intuitive sense of character timing as you watch your assemble edits. It is wise to show early cuts of the film to other people and ask for feedback. Ask if they lose track of a character that doesn't appear often enough or feel overwhelmed by one who appears too often. Your task is to keep a balance as the story unfolds.

Relationships

Characters exist in a world of relationships. They interact with each other, and with other elements in a story. To identify these relationships, simply ask yourself, "What are the characters' relationships to each other?"

As you find relationships, look for visual metaphors to represent them. In *Why Do These Kids Love School?* a jewelry teacher places a little girl's hands on a tool, and tugs on the wire to allow the child to feel the tension.

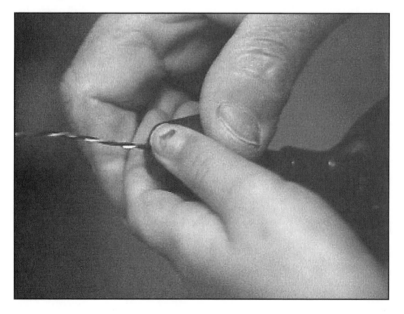

As the teacher steps back, the camera focuses on small hands, doing the work. This image depicts the relationship between the teacher and child, and how the teacher gives this child control as she learns a new task.

Conflict

In order to achieve a sense of moving forward, there need to be restraints and challenges that the characters overcome, push past, break through, or transcend. Difficulties create conflict for the characters, and conflict is the essence of drama.

In *The Fragile Promise of Choice*, when we hear that the Catholic Church objects to women seeking safe abortions, even if these women are poverty stricken and desperate, that restriction presents a restraint. Then we hear Rachel, who provides safe abortions to poor Catholic Latinas, describe her sense of loss at being excommunicated from the Catholic Church because of her work. The viewer feels her sadness, and the conflict becomes palpable. When she straightens herself and sits upright and says with conviction, "But, this is not going to silence me, I will speak out," you can feel the resolution within this drama. She is not going to be defeated.

When you show conflict in your film, internal or external, present it without editorializing. Let the conflict speak for itself. If you clearly take a position, the audience may feel pressured and pull back. If you are using interviewees, let them speak of their own realizations and breakthroughs.

My current film project is called *Stealing America: Vote by Vote*. Today I committed to a shooting trip in the Blue Ridge Mountains of Georgia. When we're done in Georgia, we'll be going to Florida to interview a candidate who is certain his election was stolen.

He has been going door-to-door to collect affidavits from people who voted for him, in order to prove that not all the votes for him were counted. His results are proving that he was right.

In the film, activists, like this man, describe the ways that they are fighting for voters' rights. They describe their anger at seeing long crowds of voters waiting in line for up to fourteen hours on Election Day. Some of the interviewees were in those lines.

At first, the situation seems virtually impossible to fix. However, as the activists speak about their commitment to election integrity, the viewer sees that their efforts lead to personal triumphs as they break through barriers and take action.

These people, not a narrator, tell that story in their own words.

WHEN A "CHARACTER" IS NOT A PERSON

Sometimes key "presence" in a film is not a human being. In *Radiance*, the lead character is Light itself — spiritual Light, physical light, and the light of insight.

When I began this film, some people tried to discourage me, and told me that I probably could not make a successful film about an abstract subject like Light. But to me, Light had a life of its own, beyond what just meets the eye.

I began by reading everything I could find about the nature of light — ranging from accounts of religious and spiritual encounters with an ineffable luminous force to scientific research about the effects of photons on insects. I learned that descriptions of experiences of light spanned thousands of years, and showed up in spiritual practices across the planet.

My research provided building blocks with which to construct the story. I found ways to describe the "character" of spiritual light.

The challenge was how to show this phenomenon across recorded history, as well as in everyday life.

Light, as a "character," led me to images ranging from ancient religious art to soaring cathedrals to macro-photography of flowers to shimmering special effects to evocative music (chanting Tibetan monks, a church choir singing J. S. Bach, eerie synthesizer music followed by gentle lyric acoustic guitar and more), and minimal narration.

The timing between sequences while editing was critical. I needed to let each layer unfold in a way that allowed the viewer to not only follow but take the journey. *Radiance: The Experience of Light* is alive and well, thirty years after I made it! I just checked on the Internet and it has been viewed eight thousand times and downloaded by more than two thousand people. It's been up on the Internet for less than two years!

http://www.archive.org/details/radiance

If you are doing an issue-driven, essay style documentary, the issues themselves are your "characters." You will need to identify and flesh out the issues as the spine of your story.

A good example of an issue-driven documentary is *Berkeley in the Sixties* (1990), by Mark Kitchell. What you need to find to develop issues such as freedom of speech and racial discrimination is archival or current day footage that brings the issues to life, and gives them reality.

Other Elements of Story

Some of the other major pieces you will be working with when you build your story are settings, trajectory and pacing.

The Setting

All stories exist in one or more settings. Every story begins someplace, moves through that space, sometimes to another place, and arrives in a place where the story ends. In a film these places can be a physical space, a state of mind, or a fantasy place.

Settings will influence your story profoundly. For example, a story that takes place in Hawaii amid the surfing culture with giant waves rolling onto white sand beaches or the rural fields of India will be a profoundly different than a story that takes place in a dim alley of an urban slum or a tiny crowded repair shop in Menlo Park, California.

The challenge in filming a setting is to make the story come alive to someone who was not there. As you study a setting, look for the details that give the story dimensionality and move the story forward. On a Hawaiian beach, for example, the detail could be a tiny crab scurrying under a rock, or the fast-moving face of a massive wave.

Characters tend to "belong" in certain settings. Most commonly, the place is simply where a person lives or works, which may or may not be visually interesting. Sometimes, however, you want to find another setting. Once you've filmed a character in one setting (indoors, outdoors, at work, at play, etc.), you might want to shoot that same character in a new setting as a backdrop. Or, you may choose to film "cover footage" of places where they've never been, to help flesh out a "feel" for their story. A nursery schooler may have never been to college, but you might show a college campus if you are talking about the child's educational future. As you work with settings — whether choosing them or filming them — ask yourself:

Where do your characters need or want to be? Or, what settings would make good B-roll and "cover" for this interviewee? If one setting seems incongruous or limiting, where else might they belong? And if they are not in the right place, is that part of their struggle?

Your characters may move through several settings or stay in one place. You might spend the entire story in one location and get to know the details, or move through other locales and arrive someplace completely new.

For Molly Hale's story, I wanted to show the variety of settings in which she became stronger and learned to walk again. The locations include her home, the therapy swimming pool, the stable where she rides horses, the rehab center where she exercises, the forest where she and Jeramy go to get away from it all, and the park where she plays with a neighbor child.

In the Ethiopia AIDS series, one of the composite characters is "groups of men." We meet soldiers in their training camps, truck drivers at truck stops, and farmers who gather in a large mud hut on farmlands.

While most characters in my films start out where they live and/or work, if the role they play goes beyond that community, I may choose a setting outside of that venue.

To make a sweeping statement about the emerging struggle for women's rights in Ethiopia, we visited a rural province, where women from across the country gathered to make a public statement about ending violence against women. Dressed in a rainbow of traditional ethnic dresses, they gathered in a vast open field, drumming, dancing, singing, and snaking their way forward as they chanted their plea to be treated with greater dignity. That "setting" was a metaphor for their vision for themselves.

Trajectory

The trajectory — the direction in which the story is heading — is another major element. As your characters move through the story, and go from one place to another, whether psychologically or physically, there needs to be a reason for them to exist and then move forward, or backwards. Where are they going and why?

One of the Ethiopian women, a sex worker at night, is shown learning to become a baker during the day. Another woman, a social worker, who had little understanding of a sex worker's life in her own past, comes to realize that most of the sex workers are trying to feed their children. She opens her heart and her mind to these women who are struggling to survive. We experience how each of these women is growing and changing.

Visually, in the film, we actually see the sex worker baking, and we see the social worker going through the narrow alleyways of Addis Ababa to meet with the women she is helping to start new lives.

Pacing

These changes cannot happen instantly. They need time. The sex worker reflects on her life first, and as she does, she pours batter onto the sizzling griddle, while learning to bake the pancake-like bread *injera*, which is a part of every Ethiopian meal. The social worker speaks of earning the trust of the women as she gets to know each of them, one by one.

As each character grows, the story evolves.

WHERE DO YOU WANT TO TAKE THE VIEWER?

As you build the story, you must constantly ask yourself where you want the viewer to go. Is it a physical journey from one place to another, or is it an internal journey? In *Why Do These Kids Love School?* it is a chronological journey, as we move from nursery school through eighth grade graduation.

As the filmmaker, you have the responsibility to decide what kind of response you want the audience to feel. Where do you hope the viewer will go with the story? From frustration to peace? From passivity to activism? From ignorance to insight?

In what direction does your story pull the viewer? Every good story has an emotional undertow created by the images and people that run through the scenes. This undertow creates a "pull" that draws the viewer into the film. Your job is to edit together a story that has that pull, but without people feeling they are being manipulated. How do you do this? Let the story tell itself. No forcing, just unfolding. You want to be able to convey the truth at the heart of your story without needing to explain it, without telling the viewer what to think or feel.

Ask yourself, how do you want the viewer's perception to change, or not change, by the end of this journey, through watching your film? Asking this question will help you put together what will be needed to get there.

The process of building a story is complicated. What brings the pieces together? Sometimes it is your intuition, sometimes it is feedback from friends and other filmmakers, sometimes it is juxtaposition of information. Often it is interviewees who say something that changes the direction of story and brings a new dimension into focus, as did a sex worker I interviewed one evening in Ethiopia.

My cameraman and I gingerly made our way, sometimes skidding down a steep alley running off a back street in Addis Ababa. It was pouring rain and we were frantically trying to keep the equipment as dry as possible. When we arrived at our destination, a one-room hut, we were greeted warmly by a commercial sex worker and her friends. The first thing they did was wash my feet with water they'd carried from a community pump. I will never forget the gentle care they used.

After welcoming us, the host settled herself on a mattress which covered most of the floor of her one room. As soon as the camera was rolling, she told us horror stories: of how she was abused by customers; of how men stole money from her after sex; of how she and other women were threatened and beaten if they wouldn't have sex without a condom.

Gradually, after she'd shared a series of painful memories, the stories shifted. She began to describe how she was learning to protect herself — from abuse and from becoming infected — and how she was teaching other sex workers to take care of themselves.

When I had first come to her, I only expected to hear stories about how sex workers in this culture were downtrodden. I wanted to create a compassionate portrait, to show that they were victims of a gender-biased system. I hadn't known, until that night, how much the sex workers themselves were being trained and helped to help each other. The film we produced about women in Ethiopia from various walks of life, follows the progression of that evening — from suffering and struggling against all odds, to learning new skills, and then becoming teachers to each other.

I found myself here on another continent, a thousand miles from India, and many thousand from California, continuing a journey I had started with a trilogy on abortion rights many years earlier, of women stepping forward and speaking out.

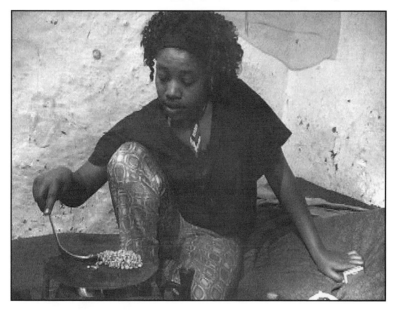

KEY POINTS

- The story building process begins in preproduction and continues through shooting, editing, and feedback screenings.

- As characters move through your film, your job is to show their growth.

- All characters exist in a world of relationships. Through your film you can show the audience how characters relate to each other, even if they don't know each other.

- Conflict is the heart of drama.

- To achieve a sense of moving forward, your characters must overcome obstacles.

- Obstacles and conflicts can be physical, mental, emotional, or spiritual, but whatever they are, you must find a way to make them palpable.

- It takes different kinds of resources to build a story in film: the creative ability to tell a story, and the skills to edit the elements together into an engaging film.

- Your job is to convey the truth at the heart of the story to the viewer, and keep the viewer's interest while doing so.

- As you build the story, you must constantly ask yourself, "Where do I want the viewer to go?"

CHAPTER 15

EDITING

1. As the filmmaker, your job is to weave together the elements: footage, stills, interviews, sounds, music.

2. Begin by putting everything you need in the computer, and then print it out on paper.

3. Log all your footage, and transcribe the interviews you will be using in the film.

4. As you review the footage, watch for moments that touch you emotionally. Those moments are the same ones that will "grab" an audience.

5. Clarify your working arrangements with your editor, from the first day.

6. Some of the best editing happens late at night, on weekends, or near dawn — times when you can work undisturbed for long periods.

Every element in a documentary film has its own function — interviews, A-roll, B-roll, narration, music, sound effects — the magic is in how these juxtapose and fit together. It is the filmmaker's job to oversee the interaction of these elements.

The Elements of a Documentary Film

A-roll footage is sync sound footage which adds to the story, often footage of an interviewee doing something which can be used to "cover" cuts in his or her interview.

B-roll is footage that shows the events, situations, people, or things that the interviewee or narrator are describing.

Cutaways are often details within the environment. For example: the interviewee's hands, a memento or a keepsake, a picture or diploma, anything specific in the interviewee's environment.

Cover footage is general footage that shows the atmosphere of a place, situation, person, or event you are filming. For example: a street scene in the city where you are filming, or an establishing shot of the building where the interview is taking place.

For this chapter, assume you are the Director. Someone else may do the job for you, but for now, be the Director. As the Director, certain decisions are yours alone. When I refer to "editor," I understand it also might be you, or an editor you hire, or a team consisting of you and the editor.

As the Director, you have to make this film your own unique project. You will incorporate everything you've learned, achieved, and acquired during production experience and actually, during your life!

You have to hold your vision steady, while simultaneously allowing it to evolve. Whatever originally inspired you to make this film might become elusive as the film progresses.

The editing room is where you put it back together, sift and sort, and weave together elements as you build the story. This is where the filmmaker re-claims the vision and breathes life into the story. In the editing, even if someone else does the hands-on part, you are creating a new reality that will have "your touch."

When I was making *Radiance*, my editor and I watched translucent jellyfish pulse across the small screen above the Steenbeck 16mm film editing deck. The jellyfish were luminous, as sunlight streamed through their bodies. This was a perfect image for a film about light, but something didn't feel right, something about the rhythm and how they moved with the music.

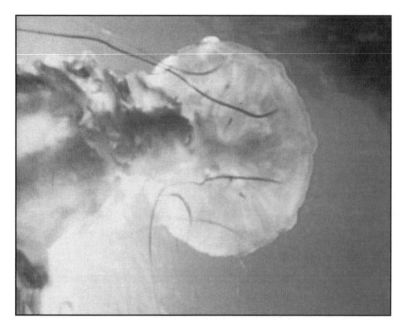

After I watched those images over and over, I began to feel what needed to happen. The sudden movements of the jellyfish as they thrust forward seemed abrupt. I wanted their movements to feel more sensuous. I realized the jellyfish should be slowed down!

I did some research, and learned about "step printing" 16mm film, in which there are two identical frames for each single frame. I learned that it was an expensive process. Some people urged me not to spend my small budget that way, others told me not to tamper with the rhythms of nature.

But I had an inner sense of what the film needed. So, I raised more money, and paid hundreds of dollars (1977 dollars) to "step print" the footage. It worked beyond my expectations. As the audience first enters the film, I invite them — by slowing down the jellyfish — to "enter" another reality.

When you set out on the editing process, you start with a road-map — the story you thought you were going to tell. But this map isn't the whole picture. The map doesn't show you who lives in the countryside, what the trees look like, or where the farms are along the way. You only learn what the countryside is really like when you take the journey. The feel of the story is built in the editing room as you watch the footage and see what works and doesn't work.

WEAVING THE THREADS TOGETHER

Whether you do the editing yourself, or you bring in an editor, be realistic. If you look at the shelves (or boxes) full of tapes and discs, the files full of papers, and the stacks of images to be scanned or filmed and think, "This is overwhelming!" you'll simply get depressed.

So, go one step at a time

The Major Steps in the Editing Process

In my way of working, the editing and story-building process are interactive and they inform each other. To some extent these steps are a review of Chapter 14, Building the Story.

1. Log the footage: interviews, synch-sound scenes and B-roll.

2. Capture as you log, or capture the strongest material after it is logged.

3. Transcribe the interviews.

4. Identify the strongest parts of the interviews (selects).

5. Using the selects, lay out different ways the story might take shape. This can be done on paper, with filing cards or in the computer.

6. Make a sketch of an "assemble edit" with pieces of paper or cards attached and laid out on a "story board" or a big table, or do this in the computer by cutting and pasting.

7. Put together several versions of a rough cut of the film.

8. Get feedback on these rough cuts.

PREPARING FOR THE EDIT

The key to efficient editing is preparation. It's important to have all your materials organized before you start putting your story together. That means labeling all your tapes and discs, logging your footage, making careful notes, filing everything neatly, and creating orderly computer files and folders.

Logging Your Footage

Logging is how you organize and identify all of your footage. The logs must be complete and comprehensive so that the editor can keep track of and find whatever is needed. Depending on how you set it up, the logging may be done by you, your editor, or an intern.

The person doing the logging must watch all of the footage and record a simple description of each short segment or scene or shot, and note any additional relevant information about that piece of footage. Plan on taking at least three hours to log one hour of footage.

Information to Record When Logging

Tape numbers and names

Basic description of footage

Description of what is shown and said in each shot or sound bite

In-points and out points (hour: minute: second: frame) of each scene, shot, and sound bite

Time code: at least three times on each page of interview

Additional information

Identify especially moving scenes or those with important information

Technical quality of images

Technical quality of sound

ETHIOPIA PROJECT LOGS
Tape #: 01.3C2 Mary Joy: neighborhood coffee ceremony HIV/AIDS lecture

Quality Rating (1-4)	Name of shot	Time Code	Log Note
2	Woman cooking beans	In: 01:00:59;12 Out: 00:00:49;23	MS Woman in black body wrap/scarf seated on low wood bench, stirring coffee beans. Mud wall and wood door in BG.. Cups, tray, implements in front of her.
2	Woman cooking beans 1	In: 01:01:49;04 Out: 00:01:36;02	MS Slightly further back of woman in black body/head scarf stirring coffee beans as they cook. She speaks to someone off camera at end of shot. Airplane audible in middle of shot
3	Woman cooking beans 2	In: 01:03:25;05 Out: 00:00:35;07	MS Woman in black cooking coffee beans. Man enters on left sits. Woman walks in front of camera, sits partly visible on right. Camera zooms back, then closer.
3	Woman cooking beans 3	In: 01:04:00;11 Out: 00:05:13;09	WS Group of women in white body scarves, men, seated around woman in black cooking coffee beans. Dirt ground; green bldg. In BG. Men on left in FG glances occasionally at

Transcribing Interviews

If you walk into the editing room (or space) of a documentary filmmaker, you will usually see binders filled with transcriptions of interviews. Some documentary filmmakers transcribe every interview themselves, which gives them a better understanding of the characters and helps them remember what interviewees say. My own preference is to work with volunteers to do transcription. I am a slow typist and I find the task overwhelming. Also, I like to involve others, when possible, with straightforward tasks.

Whether you do the transcriptions yourself or not, make sure that whoever does the transcription enters time code frequently so you can easily find the source of an interview.

Transcribing Sync Sound Scenes (A-roll)

I also transcribe selected portions of meetings, interactions such as a conversation between important characters, and other key scenes I might use. These are not interviews, but what is said or what happens might be relevant to your story.

The Paper Edit

The "paper edit" is a standard filmmaking tool that allows filmmakers to visualize a film and organize their material. One way to do it is by making copies of all the transcripts and then snipping out the best bits (with each bit identified by time code) and pasting them onto another sheet of paper, or board, in the order that the viewer will see the footage when it is edited together.

I generally do a paper edit for the first cut of the film. Some filmmakers just assemble by instinct and put together a first pass on the computer "by feel."

Try an Audio Edit Instead of a Paper Edit

When Paul Crowder edited *Riding Giants*, he assembled the audio clips from their best scenes into what he called a "radio version" of the story.

Using director Stacy Peralta's highlighted transcripts, Crowder assembled the audio clips on a time line in his editing system.

Then, Crowder and Peralta listened to the sound clips as if they were listening to a radio show.

Only when they were satisfied with the radio version, did they begin to edit the images.

Riding Giants (2004), Stacy Peralta.

To make a paper edit, first watch the tapes with copies of the transcripts in hand. Highlight the strongest bites on the printed out transcripts. Your goal is to create a working version of a possible "script" in which you can move the pieces around. Several approaches:

- Cut the best bites out of the transcripts, and tape them onto blank pages in a three-ring binder or

- Fasten them to a story board or

- Cut and paste them into a new document in the computer and print out this trial ordering of interview bites and sync sound scenes.

Your Work Schedule

Some people can work intensely twelve or more hours a day. Other people need to work regular hours, eight hours a day. If you normally work long hours, don't expect the staff (especially your editor) to follow you in your mode of working. The editor, in trying to please you, might burn out from exhaustion and you will have lost more than you gained.

HANDS-ON EDITING

Many books and courses on digital editing exist. What I'd like to go over here is not the detailed mechanics or techniques of editing but instead, your process.

The "Assemble Edit"

An assemble edit is a quick assembly of the scenes and bites that you've identified as "keepers." The purpose of an assemble edit is to get a gestalt of what you have so far, and to see where you need to make changes. A storyboard may or may not precede this step.

To make an assemble edit, stitch together the best scenes and interview bites in your computer, without regard to length, sound, B-roll, or missing footage. When you watch the assemble edit, you will begin to see which scenes play together well, which scenes need to be cut, and where you need to add footage.

The first assemble edit may not look anything like your final film. But trying out story lines is a way to get started, with the understanding that characters, and even whole scenes, may appear or disappear as you go forward.

To keep track of the changes, be sure to update your storyboard whenever you move, add, or delete a scene.

Keep Track of Changes

Take occasional photos of your storyboard so you will have a record of the evolving story. I also find it very useful to make a script, save it by date, and edit new versions, from which I work.

Moment by Moment Transcript

real time	speaker	dialogue	cover
02:17:10	Narrator	The fifth cervical vertebrae was fractured with a dislocation between six and seven.	Still: b & w image of vertebrae
02:27:08	Jeramy	And based on the x-rays and what they saw, um, in her neck, they said, "we'll be able to take the pressure off the cord, but people don't come back from these kinds of things."	Close-up x-ray
02:43:15	Narrator	Molly Hale was an athletic woman, who practiced the martial art of aikido. She had been an architectural designer and also worked with her husband Jeremy, in the music business.	Still: Molly steering a boat. Moving footage: M & J practicing aikido. Still: b/w of Molly's hands.

Rough to Fine Cut

The rough cut is the next step after the assemble edit. It is closer to the finished film than the assemble edit, but may still lack various scenes, interview bites, cover, and music. The color may be different from scene to scene, and some of the sound may be rough or even missing. But a rough cut shows the whole form of the movie for the first time. It's closer to finished so that you can clearly see the story.

My process is one of continually reassembling, moving pieces, trying new beginnings, cutting scenes, and adding scenes. I often end up making ten or more rough-cut versions.

As you edit the rough-cut, pay attention to how the material affects you. Your feelings will act as a barometer which you can track. Whatever you feel — moved, angered, inspired — there's a good chance that your viewers will also be touched in similar ways.

Pay Attention to These Things When Editing the Rough-Cut

1. What interviewees say, and how they say it

2. How each sequence of a few minutes of footage looks and feels

3. Your reactions/responses

4. Look for — and trust — that elusive spark of truth: Stop when you see or hear something that says to you, "Pay attention!" You will sense those moments and learn to say to yourself, "Yes! That's it!"

When I am satisfied with the emotional content and information of an interview, I sometimes tighten the audio track further (if we can get in between the words) by editing out long pauses and qualifiers like "I think," or "maybe," or "well."

I also try to cut sounds like "uh" and "ah."

There are usually spaces between words — sometimes only a few frames — with which you can work to "get in there" and trim. These words and sounds tend to dampen the intensity of what someone is trying to say. By editing them out, the strength of the communication comes through with greater clarity. When you have a good sound editor, and your interviewee is covered with B-roll in the right places, you can work miracles!

During the fine cut, we craft the images and the sound. Sometimes we add pauses, sometimes we tighten the interviews and scenes to give them greater focus. When you tighten sentences and take out whole phrases, the viewer is led to concentrate on the emotional content of what is being said. As you remove unnecessary phrases, you are cutting for impact. When editing, remember that generally, "less is more."

Picture Lock

Picture lock is when the picture is set, and timing is final, and no further image edits are made.

Audio editing, after picture lock, includes tweaking sound levels, taking out pops, laying in narration and final music tracks and other sound work. Audio sweetening and the sound mix preparation all happen after the picture lock.

For a good explanation of sound I recommend the book *Sound for Digital Video* by Tomlinson Holman.

BUILDING THE STORY IN THE EDITING ROOM

You usually begin editing with an idea of what the beginning, middle, and end of the story will be. However, when you assemble the footage, you may find that one or more of these parts does not "work" in that position.

When this happens, set aside material that isn't working and focus on the scenes that do work together. Getting one piece of the story to work will often help you see what needs to happen next, and the rest of the story will start to fit together.

Once I was editing an interview with a woman who was describing her relationship with her husband. The interview was informative, but there was no vitality, until she began to talk about how he stood by her in hard times. The camera was in close, and her eyes filled with tears. What came through was the absolute love she felt for him and from him. A soft glow covered her face. One look showed the truth of what was at the heart of their relationship. That split second became the hub of a scene in the film. I might have missed that "look" had I not been open to moments that touched me. The editing room is where you can discover and then use those moments.

When you are reviewing footage, listen carefully and watch people's faces and bodies as they speak. Even people who think that their emotions are hidden, will unconsciously reveal themselves through a gesture, a facial expression, some body position, or a glance. Make a note when you see these moments. Though such instants are vivid while you are watching, you can lose track of the moment, later, unless you are sure to log it carefully.

WORKING WITH AN EDITOR

There are advantages and disadvantages to bringing in an "outside" editor. If you do the editing yourself, you can shape the film every step of the way, and craft each nuance. However, a new pair of eyes brings a fresh perspective to the material, and a new person will be able to see things you may overlook. If you decide to hire an editor, it is important to choose someone with whom you connect. When you select an editor, you want someone who can align with your purpose. But also choose someone who has a strong sense of what he or she brings. Filling this position will be one of the most important decisions you will make and can lead to the difference between an average film and a fantastic film. A good editor may challenge your thinking, and both of you have to be flexible. You have to be willing to put your egos aside (as well as you can) and collaborate.

There are various ways to work together with an editor:

- Side by side, sharing decisions
- You direct, the editor follows your direction
- You step back, and the editor cuts the film, you review cuts as the project develops

An editor's job is to help you solve problems! From the very start you should let your editor know how you like to work, and find out how your editor wants to work, then strike a balance. You need to be comfortable with each other from the beginning.

Some editors prefer to review the material and decide upon a story and a first cut without any input. Others want you to state your vision from the first meeting, and then for you to give input at every step along the way during not only first but subsequent cuts.

You need to ask yourself: How much input do you need and want from the editor? If you don't know that answer at first, be flexible about adjusting the way you are working as you go.

Depending on how you decide to work together, the first cut of the film may be the editor's interpretation. The first time you see everything — from beginning to end — might be after the editor has assembled it. On this first pass, the editor will not always "bring out" the idea you had in mind when the film was being shot.

At this point, filmmakers sometimes see every problem and every missed opportunity. One reaction to the first cut or assemble edit might be frustration or sadness. Remember:

The first cut is just a starting point, and rarely matches the film in your mind.

On the other hand, sometimes, the editor's first pass might be better than what you imagined. A skilled editor can create totally different outcomes by experimenting and rearranging the material.

If you are the writer-director-producer, sharing the story-building task with an editor is a delicate balance of deciding who is in control of which cut. What will you do if the editor cuts down your favorite character or deletes your favorite scene? Can you remain open to the fact that the editor may be right? You may need to let go of some of your favorite scenes for the overall good of the film. At other times, you need to re-assert your opinion and give the editor explicit directions. Whether you are letting go or taking back control, you have to continually listen to and trust your intuition.

Differing with the Editor

Remember that an editor is working with you, but bottom line, *for* you. It is your film. So editing is partly about trusting your intuition and not letting someone else tell you what to do or not do. Take input, but make sure it is the filmmaker's film, yours. If you are the director, it is about finding what feels right for you, and ideally, it will feel right for the editor, too.

One of the trademarks of my films is to freeze and then fade. When someone says something profound (at least something that seems profound to me) at the end of an interview bite, I often freeze the last frame and fade down rather than cut out. I like giving that moment an added beat to allow what's been said to resonate.

The first time I asked one of my editors to try this technique she said, "I really don't want to do it! It's a cheap trick!"

She thought freezing and fading was not only inappropriate for the documentary on which we were working, but "tacky" and she didn't want to do it on principle.

I insisted that she try it, and we would see. Much to her surprise, it worked really well. When I ask viewers if they saw the freeze and fade, the response is almost always, "The what? No, we didn't notice it, but whatever you did, it worked."

There is no book that tells you when to fight for your vision and when to compromise. Each filmmaker has to develop a special feeling for the material and develop relationships that make it possible to bring that vision into form.

Letting the Material Speak

Try to approach the story without preconceptions. Ask yourself, "What can I learn from this material? What is it trying to say?"

When you approach editing with this attitude, you are able to hear the voices of the people in the film. This way of working helps you avoid the temptation to force the material into the story you wanted to tell from the beginning. Be open to letting the story tell itself.

When I am editing, I need to keep remembering to give the material space, and allow it to unfold in the way it wants to unfold, at the right pace: not too fast, and not too slow, and very important, not too dense. I say to myself, "Let it breathe!"

CRAFTING THE STORY

Pacing

The pacing determines how a viewer will be drawn into your movie. There are many ways to affect the pace. You may imagine that a barrage of quick cuts will draw the viewer into the film, but these may surprise you and push the viewer back. A series of dissolves may coax the viewer deeper into the story or slow things down. A pause may serve to invite the viewer into the scene in a way that is subtle, yet insistent. It may also create boredom. Sometimes the most effective way to work with a scene is to do nothing. Just let it run for a while.

Whatever you do, or don't do, will affect the pacing. When you are working with the pacing you need to check in and ask yourself where you want the story to slow down and unfold, speed up and intensify, space out and breathe, or some combination of these.

Juxtapositions

Juxtaposing two elements, and then watching what happens, is one of the delights of filmmaking. When juxtaposition is done well, you end up with a sequence that is captivating. For the Peninsula School film, which shows a carefree wildness indoors and out, I used a soundtrack of simple structured classical piano music by Bach and Mozart. The juxtaposition of free-flowing activities and the orderliness of the music create an intricate interaction in which the elements together create a dynamic whole.

FINDING YOUR STYLE

Getting in "The Zone"

For many of us, the best editing happens late at night or on the weekends, when you can build a time capsule around yourself. For me that happens at dawn. It is hard to create this space when the phone is ringing, or someone is saying "Come take a look at this." When you are in a bubble of privacy, you have the time and space to concentrate exclusively on the flow of the material, the job of editing and to allow your inspiration to rise.

As you get closer to the final cut, the people around you will have their own ideas about what they want you to do. While you want feedback from others, at the same time you need to reaffirm that this is your project. When you get input from others, take charge and decide what is in and what is out, and a thousand other decisions that will determine the final feel of your film.

Your Touch

Editing is the essence of your style as a filmmaker. It is the place where a film student becomes a filmmaker. It is where you mark your territory.

Intuition is an enormous part of editing. Your goal must be to sense how to engage the viewer, and sustain that interest while telling your story. Develop the habit of keeping the viewer in mind while editing. Might you lose the viewer when you make an abrupt cut? Or is the pace dragging? People can become bored in a split second. You learn these things about what works and doesn't work by getting honest feedback as you show the works-in-progress. Then, when you go back to the editing room, you can try your hand at new approaches.

There are any number of stylistic possibilities, such as quick cuts, slow dissolves, or a montage of stills, which might fulfill your need for a certain "feel." Ideally, you are able to coordinate a kind of conversation between the footage, your preferences, your imagined viewer's response, and how you bring these together.

There is only one brass ring to catch on the merry-go-round of filmmaking — the one with your name on it. Your style will reflect what you want to say and how you say it. Even if you have an editor, the vision rendered should be yours. Two different people will make two completely different films from identical material.

After all is said and done, editing is a continuous dance. It is a dance between your vision, the editor's vision, the images, and the audio. When you are successful at this dance, people will tell you that they remember your films.

KEY POINTS

- As a director, you face certain challenges during editing — making the film uniquely yours and sustaining your original vision, while, at the same time, letting go of what doesn't work.

- As you edit, listen carefully to interviewees, and watch their body language and facial expressions.

- One of the most important decisions you will make on the film is whether to bring in an editor and if you do, how to work together.

- Clarify who, between you and your editor, will make which editing decisions before you begin editing.

- It is in the editing room that you (and perhaps an editor) breathe life into the film.

- Some of the best editing happens when you build a time capsule around yourself. That might be late at night, at dawn, or on the weekends

CHAPTER 16

FEEDBACK SCREENINGS

1. *You get to decide everything that goes into your film,
   but you don't get to decide whether the film has impact.
   The audience decides that.*

2. *At each point along the way, your feedback screenings
   will have a different purpose.*
   - *Early screenings — to see how people respond to the
     individual interviewees and scenes*
   - *Middle screenings — to shape content and assess
     length*
   - *Final screenings — to craft the completed film before
     release*

There are different kinds of feedback screenings that will let
you know, as you are making the film, what the potential audience response might be.

We held an early feedback screening for my film about education in a cavernous room in a converted warehouse. Thirty or
so filmmakers showed up to see the work-in-progress which
at this point had no narration, no cover, just footage that told
the story.

At least I thought it told the story.

The first comment was a blunt question, "What is this film
supposed to be about?"

My heart began to sink. One by one, others asked variations of
that question. They were supportive of me, but very critical of
the film. I soon realized that because I understood the subject
well, I had assumed that the meaning of the film was obvious.
Until that "assemble edit" feedback screening, I could not see

that the film wasn't working. What seemed crystal clear to me, appeared as a confusing jumble of ideas to the viewers. That feedback screening was invaluable!

The final version, which became a prime time PBS special, used narration throughout, to guide the viewer through a maze of complex approaches and some subtle points about progressive education.

A Reality Check

Feedback screenings, when presented thoughtfully, provide a reality check. Even though you may think you are communicating well, you will get a new level of objective input when other people see your work early on and give you their candid impressions.

If you want to create a truly powerful film, I strongly suggest submitting the work-in-progress for review: to friends, strangers and people who care about the topic. Otherwise the film will have just your perspective, and that is usually not enough.

Stages of Feedback

Early Screenings

Soon after we shoot the first interviews for a film, I call together a few people to screen the footage. I ask them to be candid: "I want your honest opinions of these interviewees. I have not decided yet who is in and who is not. Who engages you? Who feels believable or unbelievable to you? Does anyone bore you?" Then I ask, "Can you say why you think you react that way?"

If people can be specific, that helps you understand why a person or a scene may need to be dropped. Does an interviewee have mannerisms of speech that interfere with people's attention? Is a scene too confusing and do people get lost?

Early screenings are not as much about content as they are about feeling. If the story is not engaging yet, I continue to move the pieces around until it is. I don't work on the story in detail until I find the elements that will be most effective.

During this process, the core vision will probably remain intact, but the way the story is being told will evolve.

Middle Screenings

In middle screenings, you have a story, but it will continue to change as you focus on the content of the film. You make content changes when you find that audiences want more information, or report that the story line seems too slow. At these screenings, I also ask things like: "Is it too short, is it too long? If so, where? Did you get confused? if so, where?"

Final Screenings

In the later screenings, you are asking for suggestions that will be used to make subtler changes, to sand and shape the film. You may change the pacing in subtler ways. You may find that certain scenes still don't work yet and need to be tweaked or certain characters need to be cut down, or even out.

I'm looking for "splinters" at this point, small things that stick out and keep the film from working as well as it could.

LOGISTICS

To hold a feedback screening you need to:

- Find a venue
- Invite attendees
- Create a feedback form/questionnaire
- Review the forms after the screening

The Venue

Small feedback screenings can be very effective. You may only want to invite five or six people to come together and review the work in progress. The best space for intimate screenings is someplace quiet and comfortable, perhaps in your own or a friend's home. At the other end of the spectrum, more than once, I have held feedback screenings in a theater that holds more than three hundred people.

The best time to hold a feedback screening is on a weekday evening. During the day people generally work and go to school, weekends they often have other plans. One and a half to two hours from start to finish is a good length. Test all the audio-visual equipment before people arrive, including the TV and VCR, or computers and projector. Remember the "rule of screenings," *anything you do not test might not work properly.*

The Attendees

Friends and family are usually the easiest people to reach. They may not be as objective as certain target groups, but they are fine for a first pass. They will be supportive and they will catch glaring problems.

Potential users are the next group to consider, people who will be showing the finished film in meetings, classes, or conferences.

Theatrical screenings may be down the line, but first get your film to work!

You may hesitate to show an unfinished film yet to those who will use it when it is done, because you are afraid they will be too judgmental at this early stage. Generally, the opposite is true. If the film has at least a story and a shape, and you invite them to be part of your process, they will feel privileged to give input. They want you to succeed. Generally, they love it even more when it is finished, because they have a vested interest.

Donors are another good choice for feedback also. They've invested in the film and in you, and they will usually be honored to be asked for their opinions.

The time to invite the larger public to feedback screenings (if you decide to do that) is during the final screenings, after you have worked out most of the problems. Ideally, these people will be representative of the wider audience you hope to reach.

The Feedback Screening

You can get extremely valuable information at any feedback screening, information that will help you craft a successful film. But the only way you can take full advantage of that information is if you are willing to listen to honest criticism.

The Screening

The way you introduce the film at a feedback screening will, in part, influence the kind of feedback you get. First, tell people that you want to hear the truth, what they really think. Assure them they don't have to worry about hurting your feelings. Be clear in asking them for what you want.

In an early screening where you may be showing only interview footage, or a very early rough cut, tell the people in attendance that you are looking for feedback on the feeling of the individual interviewees or scenes, perhaps the story in general. Ask them to save their comments about the content and how it fits together for a later screening.

In a middle screening, you might have a rough cut of something to show. Ask people to comment on the length or the pace. Does the ending work? Do the transitions work? Ask them to be specific about those parts of the film that might be confusing, as well as those parts that touch them or give them hope.

In a pre-release screening or later screenings, tell the audience that the film is nearly finished, that you want feedback on the overall feeling, as well as transitions and whatever doesn't work. During the screenings, watch the audience. When you lose their attention, people will start shifting in their seats. When they are engaged, they sit still, focused on the screen.

After the screening, before you have any discussion, ask people to fill out questionnaires before they leave. If they cannot do so, ask them to mail the filled-out forms to you as soon as possible.

For any screening, no matter what size, postpone verbal feedback until the forms are turned in. You want people to write their candid first impressions, uninfluenced by other opinions. If the audience is large or the subject of your film is controversial, you may not want to open the floor for discussion at all. Instead, arrange to get detailed feedback later in small groups or individually.

If you do choose to let the feedback take place in an open forum, be prepared for the possibility that not all of the comments you get will be appreciative. Some input may be harsh. You may or may not want this to happen in a larger group. There are, however, graceful ways to deal with that. If you feel that someone is attacking you or the film, listen politely, thank them for their input. As much as possible, avoid getting defensive. You might say something like, "Thank you. That is hard for me to hear, but I am still grateful to get that input."

Keep the discussion on the short side, about a half hour. A few people will always have other commitments and leave early. Don't take that personally.

As you wrap up the discussion, tell people you'll be available afterwards (if you are) for anyone who wants to stay and talk more about the film.

Remind people to turn in their questionnaires before they leave.

The Questionnaire

The best way to get input you can review easily later is to use a questionnaire. When you write the questionnaire for a screening, keep it as concise and direct as possible. Keep "essay" questions to a minimum, if at all. Narrative answers take a long time to write and a longer time to evaluate. Be sure to include space for contact information so you can thank the reviewers and invite them to the opening.

Must-have items for a screening questionnaire

- Your address, so people can send the form to you if they forget to turn it in at the end of the screening.

- A space for their contact information so you can get in touch with them later.

Examples of questions

- Interviewees. List the principal interviewees with multiple choices for each person such as: engaging, informative, boring, irritating.

- Scenes: List the major scenes, and for each scene ask: length: too long, just right, or too short?

- Music: (if you have a scratch music track): too fast, too slow, too much, too little. Do the instruments feel right? Suggestions for other kinds of music?

- Narration: too much, just right, or too little?

These are just suggestions. The clearer you are about what you ask, the more useful the feedback will be.

SAMPLE FEEDBACK FORM FOR A FILM ABOUT ELECTION INTEGRITY
1. Overall length: too short   just right   too long

2. Balance of interviewees
   Male/female balance _____
   Age balance _____
   Ethnic/racial groups balance _____

3. Comment on each of these sections (circle one for each sections)
   a.   Before voting begins - the excitement, the long lines, not enough machines:
        too short   just right   too long

   b.   Votes flipping/switching and fading
        too short   just right   too long

   c.   Analysis of computer vulnerability
        too short   just right   too long

   d.   Exit polls
        too short   just right   too long

   e.   Disenfranchisement of minorities
        too short   just right   too long

   f.   The silence of the media
        too short   just right   too long

   g   Election reform is not a partisan issue
        too short   just right   too long

   h.   Paper ballots
        too short   just right   too long

4. Any person or subject that you think should be cut from the film?

5. Any person or subject that you think should be added to the film?

6. Your overall response to the film:

PLEASE USE REVERSE SIDE TO WRITE ADDITIONALCOMMENTS. THANKS!

INTEGRATING FEEDBACK

When integrating the feedback, look for trends in the responses. If a majority of the viewers express concern about something, it's undoubtedly a problem you should address.

There are times when you have to ignore some responses from a feedback screening. Examples:

When certain audience members are clearly biased against the content;

When someone is asking you to change the meaning of what you intend;

When you don't have access to or can't afford what is being suggested.

KEY POINTS

* You can trust feedback audiences to recognize places in a film that need work.

* To get honest feedback, make it clear you want the truth, not flattery.

* The most valuable comments are those which are very specific.

CHAPTER 17

FINISHING THE FILM

1. *An unfinished film can become an overwhelming burden that haunts you for years.*

2. *The problem of "not finishing" a work of art is extremely common, but most people don't talk about it.*

3. *Sometimes "finishing" means accepting that you'll never finish. You've changed, and the world is a different place, and it's time to let go and move on.*

4. *However, if you have an unfinished film about which you are passionate and are determined to finish, set your sights and commit to completing it.*

As hopeful as you are at the beginning, the challenges to finishing can be overwhelming. It is my hope that everyone reading this will find the energy to finish their film. However, there are times when a filmmaker "hits the wall."

This happens not only to first-timers, but to those of us who've been making films for decades.

In this chapter, we'll suggest ways to help you finish your film. But first, let's take a look at the fact that not finishing a film is not unusual.

THE PROBLEM OF "NOT FINISHING"

When I hold a "Producing with Passion" seminar, I ask the question, "Who here can imagine starting a new film?" Usually every hand goes up. Then I ask, "Who here has already started a film, but hasn't finished it?" One by one, some with embarrassment, people raise their hands and admit they are "carrying around" an unfinished film.

When I ask who has finished a film, and hasn't released it, a few other hands go up. It seems that for whatever reason, many people have been unable to complete or release a certain film. Many hopeful first-time filmmakers simply drop the film instead of finishing it. Some finish it, but have never shown or released it.

I've also learned, from these workshops and conversations with other artists, that in almost every field, people carry around incomplete projects.

Filmmakers are like many other artists who don't want to release an "imperfect" work. But as any longtime filmmaker can tell you, you never feel that it's perfect. There's always more you can do. At some point, you simply stop improving it.

There is no escape from the fact that, in most cases, if you start a film and don't finish it, or finish it and don't show it, the film doesn't "go away." There's a feeling of incompleteness that lives on; some people report that a half-finished film project haunts them.

Making a film is extremely seductive. You want to give it everything you've got — you pour more and more money into it, you spend evenings and weekends working on it. This incessant pull often takes a toll — on your relationships at home, with your colleagues, and sometimes your body.

Making *Radiance* almost cost me my marriage. After fifteen years of being genuinely happy together, my husband and I almost split because of my obsession with trying to perfect that film.

While I was trying to finish *Why Do These Kids Love School?* I developed serious digestive problems. The "completion process" had been going on for six years at that point.

Since then, I am much better able to balance my life, my relationships, my health, and my work, relatively speaking.

But it is still very hard for me to reason with myself while I am in the middle of a film, especially when I am trying to finish one.

Some filmmakers might feel guilty, because they have taken money to make a film, which they never finished — including me.

I had finished every film I ever started, except one. I shouldn't have taken it on in the first place. I didn't have the skills to make it, but I'd just come off a success. I thought, "Hey, I can do this! I'm a star!"

We worked on the film for about a year before I showed it. After the screening, in the room was dead silence. People were embarrassed for me. I'd overreached in every way and the film failed. There were too many problems to fix, so I never released that film. That was more than twenty years ago.

That film still beckons to me. Realistically, I doubt that I will ever complete it, but every so often I catch myself thinking of ways I could update it and launch it again.

The obstacles that slow you down when you are trying to finish a film come in many different shapes and sizes. Whether they are technical and logistical and involve the nuts and bolts of filmmaking, or personal, involving your emotions and beliefs, they all have one thing in common: They make it hard — if not impossible — to finish the film.

Hearts of Darkness: A Filmmaker's Apocalypse

Hearts of Darkness is the story of Francis Ford Coppola's struggle to finish *Apocalypse Now*.

As the production drags on, year after year, the viewer watches Coppola become more and more obsessed with finishing the film. *Hearts of Darkness* shows one filmmaker's compulsion to finish a film and how it affects those around him.

Hearts of Darkness: A Filmmaker's Apocalypse (1991), Eleanor Coppola, Fax Bahr, and George Hickenlooper.

People who can't finish their films tend to feel trapped. The only way to get out from under this cloud is either to finish the film or decide not to finish it and let it go.

Some good reasons to finish your film

You want to get on with your life.

You need to get the film to people who will use it when it is done, some of whom may be your funders.

You want to make other films and have to finish this one first.

Your family, your friends, your dog, your cat — they all need you back.

OBSTACLES TO FINISHING

You may have an unfinished film sitting in your closet, or on a shelf, or in a safety deposit box. If so, take heart. The obstacles that keep people from finishing films are fairly common, and they are potentially solvable.

Here are a few of the most common obstacles and some possible ways you might move forward.

Common reasons and excuses for not finishing a film

1. You don't know how to finish it, you can't figure out the right ending.

2. You are out of money, and may even be in debt.

3. You are tired and burned out.

4. Some of your best team members, who know the "project history," have moved on.

5. You are fearful of the reception the film might get.

6. You've used all your best material and there's not enough good footage to finish it properly.

7. You are afraid to finish, because you cannot imagine not working on the film.

Technical and Logistical Challenges

First let's look at the most common technical and logistical challenges filmmakers run into when trying to finish a film.

- Running out of money

- Sound and image problems that require major attention

- Permissions that are outstanding and have been difficult to obtain

- Graphics that haven't been created (yet) or you can't afford

- Getting stuck on figuring out how to produce, then producing, titles and credits

Money

One of the most common reasons to give up is when you are out of money. People (including me) often advise beginning filmmakers to raise money from friends and family, but there is a limit to what you can ask for. Friends and family are usually there to help you get started, but after that they hope you will find additional funding if you need it. They've heard about the film for a year or more, and it's getting to be "old news." Some may wonder whether the film will ever be finished.

Many filmmakers start spending their savings. When their savings are gone, they sometimes use their credit cards. I once watched a friend max out multiple credit cards. By the time he finished his film, he was in six-figure credit card debt.

Instead of going deeper into debt, look for ways to complete the film as soon and as inexpensively as possible (rather than abandoning it). Then you can release it as soon as possible so you can get on with your life.

Within any film community there exists a network of opportunities to trade services.

People may say, "You work on my film, I'll work on yours."

Also, there are many film students who simply want the opportunity to work on somebody else's real film, any film. Many of these students have good basic skills, but no films on which to practice and learn more.

Once you tap into this world, there are multiple ways to trade services or take on unpaid interns.

Some professionals, who have commercial jobs, earn enough money, and are willing to donate some time to a worthy project. Also, some freelance professionals will work on "spec." If your film makes money, they will be paid then.

Even if you manage to finish it on a shoestring budget, with volunteers, donated time and small donations, you might ask, "How can I release it without more funding?" There are now many ways to get a film out into the world for less money, rather than more. (We talk about some of these in Chapter 19.)

Sound

Sound sometimes presents a challenge when finishing a film. Filmmakers may underestimate the difficulty of getting a good soundtrack, which requires special skill and an enormous amount of work. The sound editor has a wide range of responsibilities, from "sweetening" (cleaning up and balancing the levels of the soundtracks), selecting where to place certain sounds and effects (perhaps creating some of these sounds), dividing and placing all the different types of audio into separate tracks, creating the final mix, and much more.

Getting good sound takes an artist, one with a keen ear and lots of experience, and this is generally a very expensive step in the process of finishing a film. If at all possible, find a professional to do the final sweetening and mix. If you are on a very limited budget, look for someone with experience that might do the sound for an exchange of services. Or delayed payment as "points" money if the film ever makes money. Sound carries the spirit of your work, so do not neglect to make sure you have a good soundtrack.

Permissions

The best way to approach permissions is to "do the right thing" in the beginning, and get permissions wherever required. (See Chapter 11, Preproduction Planning, for more information on permissions and releases.)

Model Releases

If you didn't get model or location releases from the people in your film when you shot the footage, try to contact the people and ask them to sign releases, whenever you can, afterwards.

Music

If you use copyrighted music you must obtain permission from the owner of the music and sometimes, in addition, other rights holders. If you don't want to do this, or can't afford permission, another option is to hire a composer to write music for your film, or else to buy some inexpensive "royalty-free" music and use it instead.

How to get royalty-free (or low-cost) music

1. Look in video magazines for advertisements for low-cost CDs of royalty-free music.

2. Look on the Web for music production libraries like Freeplay Music (*www.freeplaymusic.com*).

3. Use the royalty-free tracks which are sometimes packaged with your editing software.

4. Find a talented musician who needs a break, and ask him or her to score your film in exchange for music credits.

5. Use a program like SmartSound (*www.smartsound.com*) to make your own loops, or buy the SmartSound music library.

Archival Footage

If you need releases for archival footage you must obtain permission from the owner of the footage or his or her representative. If you don't want to do this, or can't afford permission, another option is to find some "royalty-free" footage on the Internet.

A few sources for archival and stock footage

Prelinger Archives (*www.archive.org*)

U.S. National Archives (*www.archive.gov*). The archives are so enormous that it makes sense for many filmmakers to hire a researcher. You can find out more about researchers at *http://www.archives.gov/research/hire-help/*.

Footage.net (*www.footage.net*). When you submit a request for footage on footage.net, your request is automatically forwarded to footage.net suppliers worldwide. Often, you will receive a sample and price quote by e-mail within 48 hours.

Easy Street Productions (*www.publicdomainfootage.com*). Easy Street is a large and comprehensive online source of archival and stock footage.

Another option is to re-cut your film so it doesn't require that archival footage. That approach is always a serious option for any of your expensive "incompletes."

Graphics

Graphics are a part of the filmmaking package that is often left for last. You may not know what you need or want until you have a semi-fine cut. But keep in mind that graphics may be complicated, time-consuming, and expensive. So allow time and set aside some money for creation of these images. You may be thinking about hiring someone to do computer graphics, which can be very costly.

If this task seems daunting, the best solution may be to re-cut the film so you don't need them. If you feel you absolutely need the graphics, perhaps you can look for someone who is willing to do your graphics in return for an exchange of services. That is the way most beginning filmmakers get through the jungle, by working trades.

Titles and Credits

Titles and credits often present challenges at the end of a film. If you don't yet have the final main title for your film, now is the time to choose one.

Next, you may feel that you need to design a title sequence. You might look at films similar to yours, and find a title sequence you like. Consider using it as a starting point for designing your own. If you cannot afford the fees of a professional who has done titles in the past, again, offer an exchange of services. Or, use simple titles and don't worry about being clever. Some of the most effective titles are elegant and simple.

Credits can become another reason for delay. Ideally, credits were agreed upon in a simple contract or letter of understanding with each person at the beginning of the production.

Credit problems are the penance you might have to pay for not handling this delicate subject earlier.

People who worked on the film may want and expect certain credits. You may or may not agree with them.

In the film world, credits are "money in the bank." One of my cameramen worked on a Hollywood film after his stint with me. He did all the special effects for the second unit on a film that was nominated for an Oscar. In the credits, an associate got the credit for my cameraman's work. The film won the Oscar for special effects, and as far as I know, the cameraman and his associate never spoke again. So, make sure the credits are accurate, and, if at all possible, that everyone feels good about his or her credit.

When the titles and credits are complete, make sure to double-check the spelling on all the names. It is easy to make mistakes, and one that should never happen is misspelling a name.

You do not need to get fancy with end credits either. You do not need scrolling credits. Title cards that dissolve into each other are fine, less complicated, and less expensive to create or get produced.

Personal and Emotional Difficulties

Personal and emotional obstacles come up as "blocks" for many people. If you didn't seem to have any personal or emotional problems holding you back in life when you began making a movie, having an unfinished movie hanging around your neck could be a way to cause a few. Let's look at some possible solutions.

Filmmakers struggling to complete a film report:

- Burnout
- Worrying about success

- Unresolved issues with people
- Issues with the crew
- Fear

Burnout

Finishing a film pushes many filmmakers to their physical, mental, and emotional limits. If you push too hard you might go into "burnout."

If you think you are approaching burnout, take it seriously. Don't try to "grit your teeth" and endure it. Enduring will only make things worse and heighten the tension.

If you are experiencing a serious case of burnout, take a break. You can put the film on the shelf for a few months while you get your energy back. Or, there is always the option of finishing it more quickly with whatever you've got, and releasing it sooner than you imagined you could!

Three Options If You Are Heading for Burnout

1. Stop, and take some time off. Be aware that the danger in stopping is that you may never go back to finish the film.

2. Sit down and finish it. Decide when it will be finished and resolve to have it done by that date. Then, work on nothing else until that date. On that day, you are done. Release it.

3. Give it to someone else to finish. Pay them if you have to. This may seem unsatisfying from the outside, but if your well-being is at risk, it may be the healthiest solution for you.

Unresolved Issues with the Team

An unresolved issue with someone connected to the project may prevent you from finishing the film. And even if you complete it and release the film, an unresolved personal issue may keep you from "letting go" of the film emotionally. Filmmaking can be a tough business — demanding, territorial, and hard on relationships. If you feel you've been hurt, or that you've harmed someone else, it will be a gift to yourself and your film work to forgive that person and/or yourself. You literally have to learn to let go of hurt feelings and memories of injustices. Until you let go, the relationship will linger in your mind and drain valuable creative energy from your projects in the future.

As you near the end of the film, in addition to your exhaustion, other members of the crew may feel burned out. Some may not want to stay around to finish.

You said you would be done by August, and here it is October. They may say, "I can't stay on this project any longer." They may be tired, or they may have another job waiting. I've had that happen more than once, and I had to bring in someone else to help finish.

When this happens, you just have to be fair and not make people feel guilty. The best thing to do is to set a clear date for them to complete their time with you, and then honor your agreement.

Your Own Fears and Worries

For some people, the single most overwhelming personal obstacle to finishing a film is their own fear. Fear of making a fool of yourself. Fear of disappointing the people who worked on the film, or invested in the film. Fear of failure. Fear of success. The only answer to dealing with these feelings is to work through the fear. You simply have to face and do the thing of which you are afraid. You break fear's spell by putting one foot in front of the other and going forward. Fear evaporates when you walk toward it.

You never know in advance what your film's future will be. Worrying about the film's success is a trap, especially if it keeps you from finishing.

The point is not whether your film is going to be a success or not. The point is that you have to finish it so it will have a chance.

STEPS TOWARD FINISHING A FILM

Questions to Ask

There are as many complications to finishing a film as there are filmmakers. I trust that the majority of people reading this will be able to find ways to resolve these complications and finish their films.

But I would like to give extra attention to people who are sitting with an unfinished film, or who are having difficulty finishing the one on which they are working now.

When you think about finishing your film, ask yourself this question.

"Do you really want to finish this film?"

If the answer is "No," honor that "No." It's time to put the film aside (at least for now) and move on. Free yourself from the feeling that you have failed, let go of the guilt and get on with your life.

However, if the answer is "Yes," then you might have to ask yourself another question.

"What are you willing to give up or postpone in order to finish the film?"

Decide how much time, money, and energy you are really willing to devote to finishing the film. Once you've made that decision, give that much and no more.

If you say, "I'll commit to finishing this film in one year, and I'll spend $10,000 of my own money to do it," then go for it. Tell yourself, "When the $10,000 is gone and the year is up, even if I am not finished, I will stop." Be prepared, at the same time, that you may well succeed!

Consider Not Finishing

It is healing to accept the truth of any of these things if they are true for you:

1. You may begin a film and not finish it.

2. You may make a film, finish it, and not show it to anybody.

3. You may never complete this film, or any film.

These are all okay. The important thing is to line up with what is true, and not punish yourself for being human!

The Satisfaction of Finishing

On the other hand, when someone finishes a film, wonderful things might happen.

1. People are so proud of you... and relieved.

2. The film will have a life of its own. You no longer have to baby-sit it and take it everywhere inside of yourself.

3. There are people in the film and who care about the film who will take it and show it in the world.

4. You get to go on with your life.

KEY POINTS

𐂂 There may come a point when almost every filmmaker, especially the first-time filmmaker, hits a wall when it comes to finishing a film.

- An unfinished film has a way of haunting you, and preventing you from getting on with your life.

- There are low-cost and no-cost ways to get your film out in the world.

- Signs of burnout: getting sick easily, becoming irritable, and relationship problems.

- Being honest with yourself may mean that you really don't want to or can't finish your film.

- There is great joy in finishing a film. I encourage you to do it if you can.

CHAPTER 18

WHAT'S NEXT FOR YOU?

1. Making a film changes you.

2. You may feel vulnerable and exposed if you become the focus of public attention.

3. You have a repertoire of new and valuable skills, and you have proof that you can use them successfully.

4. What now? A spectrum of options: you can make more films, become a spokesperson for your own film or the subject of your film, teach, work in a related field, or walk away from filmmaking altogether.

The day you rise to introduce your completed film to an audience, you will be a different person than when you began. Making a film changes you, sometimes in ways that are profound. The challenges you face while making a film might introduce you to your most elusive gifts, as well as some of your hidden demons. At the completion of a film project it's valuable to reflect, and ask yourself, "How has making this movie transformed me?"

When I ask myself this question, I know that I am a completely different person than I was thirty years ago — largely due to the demands of filmmaking.

I am more honest in everything I do. Though I cannot always get there, "facing the truth" has become the overarching goal in my work and in my personal life. Filmmaking has bruised me badly at times when I've tried to hide from the truth, and at the same time has given me the confidence that I need to live more honestly. I've observed that this learning curve —

this chance to learn hard lessons from my mistakes — seems to be "offered" to all independent filmmakers.

We are toughened by our failures, and strengthened by our successes, both kinds of growing prepare us "to make a difference" with our films, each in our own way.

Personal Growth

The day you complete your first film, and with each film after that, you will cross a threshold. You will have surmounted significant challenges: financial, interpersonal, technological, and much more. By the time you finish a film, you will have learned and probably re-learned many skills, including:

- How to recognize, nurture, and bring a creative vision into reality
- How to do background research
- How to select and work with a crew of strong-minded individuals
- How to write, edit, direct, and produce a movie script
- How to create and work with a budget
- How to market and distribute a film
- And finally, you will be well informed on the subject of your film

Feeling Exposed

You may feel a range of emotions inside yourself and from others after you've finished your film. People will admire you for achieving your goal and be proud of you for extending yourself. Others will be grateful that you have taken on the challenge of making a film about an important idea, one that has value.

You may also feel, and be, exceptionally vulnerable. You will be presenting the film, and yourself, in public places. You might become the subject of newspaper articles or television interviews.

If your film is controversial, you will attract both supporters and detractors. You may find yourself criticized in a way that seems unfair, in letters or even in a public forum.

When I had nationwide broadcasts scheduled for my film *When Abortion Was Illegal*, an attorney from a national "pro-life" organization sent a Federal Express letter to every PBS station in the country, warning programmers that if they showed my film without also showing a "pro-life" film (he suggested *The Silent Scream*), the stations might be practicing media bias which was against the law.

This threat was not technically accurate, because my film was not "pro-abortion" at all, but some stations became frightened and withdrew the program.

That "attack" was about the film — not me — but I've also experienced personal attacks and public mockery.

A newspaper reporter interviewed me personally about my first film, *Radiance*. He seemed appreciative during an interview, but the article, which was published the next day, belittled me, calling me "Little Merry Sunshine."

I was embarrassed and resentful, feeling that I'd been tricked by what seemed like an honest interview. Over the years, I've been able to let the negative feeling go. But now, looking back, I also understand that I was partly to blame. His article depended on my naiveté, combined with my vanity. Also, like any filmmaker, I was eager for publicity. So, I played my part. Now, I would respond differently to his invitation.

Maybe.

Just be prepared, that when you step forward with your film, you may be lauded or become a target, sometimes for the same film.

What Now?

More Films?

If you have the energy and are motivated, you might decide to make another film — perhaps on a completely different topic — or you might pursue connections you've made and go on to make another about the same or a related subject. You now have the basic knowledge and practical skills necessary to produce and put together a film on a range of subjects.

Many filmmakers do make several films on the same subject. You will have developed collegial relationships with people in the field. You may decide to cover a side of the topic that you were unable to cover in your original film. Or a subject that no one has yet covered.

Some filmmakers seem to be, at least temporarily, "done" with the subject they've tapped. They pick a completely different topic, or just take a break from filmmaking altogether. In my own case, I've done everything except take a break. I just keep on keeping on.

I've made five films on one subject, four on another, and various others that stand alone! I just keep following that inner voice suggesting to me (really telling me) what I could do next.

Teaching?

Some filmmakers turn to teaching as a "day job" to finance future filmmaking.

Tenured teaching positions are competitive and difficult to find, so many filmmakers teach part-time, in external programs, or give intensive workshops.

Some filmmakers become guest lecturers. They may show up one evening a week or once a quarter to teach a single class. At the end of the class they go home, and the rest of the week they turn their attention to filmmaking.

Those who teach in this freelance way will make some money, perhaps enough to earn a living. But there is no tenure or guarantees, so they must continue to promote themselves.

On the other hand, if you work for an institution, you will have more security, but there will also meetings, internal politics, and other bureaucratic demands. If you do decide that you want to teach at the college level and be on a faculty, you will probably need an advanced degree.

Some filmmakers decide to go back to school to gain more skills and technical knowledge, and get an advanced degree that will give them more employment options.

Becoming an Advocate?

As a filmmaker, you may have the opportunity to become a spokesperson for the subject of your film! When you make a film, you often meet and talk with experts in a given field. People within the field may now see you as an outspoken representative for something about which they care deeply.

These connections are invaluable and will go on to open many doors.

MOVING ON

You may want to call this phase of your life complete and move on. Whatever happens, whether you make another film yourself or decide to work for another filmmaker as an editor, producer, director, or cameraperson, the skills you have picked up during the making of your film are marketable.

You have joined a hardy group of individuals, filmmakers who have successfully finished a project!

You might teach, become a spokesperson, work in a related field, go on to make more films, all or none of these; the choice is yours.

KEY POINTS

- Making a film changes you.

- You now have new and valuable skills.

- You might teach, become a spokesperson or make another film.

- What comes next? The choice is yours.

CHAPTER 19

SCREENING YOUR MOVIE

1. *Screenings are useful events for educating, entertaining, encouraging fresh thinking, supporting activism, and just generally inspiring people.*

2. *Every size screening, whether small, medium, or large, has advantages and requires attention.*

3. *One of the most efficient ways to create a screening is to use an existing audience.*

4. *Screenings can be the foundation for a vigorous outreach program.*

5. *Screenings can be demanding. An effective, relatively easy alternative way to get your film seen is to put it on the Internet.*

After making a film, you may be exhausted, like a mother immediately after giving birth. Screenings of the film will help restore your energy. The responses and support of people who attend screenings of your completed movie will help you reconnect with your original vision.

Soon after the five film series about AIDS in Ethiopia was finished, I worked with my colleagues in Addis Ababa to prepare a premiere of the Amharic versions. After twenty-three hours of travel, with barely time to change clothes, I found myself "ready to go" (relatively "ready" that is). The event was to be held in a lovely small theater on World AIDS Day.

When I arrived, people were frantically running around, trying to find a projector that worked, testing different possible screens, and patching last-minute electrical connections. I was shaky from lack of sleep, and at the same time thrilled to be able to show the films in Ethiopia.

At 10 a.m., people began arriving, primarily dignitaries, men in suits and ties and women in tailored outfits. A little later, some of the interviewees began to show up, after traveling long distances from the countryside, dressed in well-washed work clothes.

The excitement continued to build. By 10:30, the room was full, with an audience of more than one hundred people.

For almost three years, I had held this image in mind, of these people coming together for a screening like this. That vision kept us going when we were overwhelmed by the task of editing films in Amharic, a language we didn't understand, with Amharic speakers by our side for every cut.

My editors almost "lost it" more than once! But they stayed for the long haul, and here we were.

We showed three films in a row, and then stopped for tea and a snack, assuming most people would then leave as they had already told me they had to go back to work. After the break, however, they all came back and stayed to see the other two films.

This labor of love, five films on AIDS in Ethiopia, had come home. They were being launched in the presence of people who would use them for years to come. Looking out into the audience, and seeing how engaged they were, I was rejuvenated.

A SPECTRUM OF PURPOSES

When I hold a screening, I am reassured that finally, often after more than a year of labor, the film is reaching people. Connecting with audiences, and the communities those audiences will reach, renews my sense of purpose.

Each screening sets into motion a message that goes out, like dropping a pebble in a pond.

I named my production company Concentric Media because, in every circle of viewers, there are always people with links to other circles. I love to travel and when I do, I show a film to as many of these circles of people as possible. Once I get it started, the film has a life of its own.

I've just returned from an eight-state tour, and while on the road for six weeks, sold five thousand DVDs of my latest film, some one at a time, some by the dozen.

When you think of potential audiences for your film, begin with the people closest to you — family, friends, crew, volunteers, and funders. Invariably, someone from among them will suggest another circle. As you screen it to the new circle, someone suggests yet another. As this process continues, the concentric circles go outward, and thousands of people you will have never met may see your film.

Reasons to Screen Your Film

Each screening will have a different purpose, usually more than one.

- To give people information, to educate
- To entertain and provide enjoyment
- To encourage people to think more deeply about a subject
- To support and inspire people in their own work
- To activate people to become involved with a cause

To Educate

Watching a film really does open people's minds to new possibilities. In the film *Fix-it Shops* we show small appliances being repaired, instead of being thrown into landfills. When we were editing, we chose footage with vacuum cleaners, toasters, and irons, common things that people use in their everyday lives. It is a gentle film, with a touch of light humor.

After the film was shown locally, the Fix-it Shop down the street had a flood of new customers. Seeing small appliances, like their own, being fixed woke people up. This is how it works when it works. Ideas that may have seemed abstract and somewhat removed become immediate and accessible.

Environmental awareness and ecological concern skyrocketed across the country following the release of *An Inconvenient Truth*, a film which gives specific examples and explains global warming and related issues in detail.

To Entertain

No matter how informational or even dry your content may seem at first, you can make it exciting. When I edited the original footage for *Why Do These Kids Love School?* I looked for moments that would draw people in, by showing children learning serious material in a way that clearly captured a child's attention. In one scene, a boy in science class is ecstatic as he watches the result of an experiment he is conducting. He

shouts, "WOW!" and starts giggling with delight as a test tube filled with vinegar and baking soda bubbles over, while he is learning about chemical reactions. This school's approach to "learning through doing" can be observed, and felt, in one joyful moment in an image.

To Encourage Fresh Thinking

Ideally, the material, even though intended to deepen people's understanding of a subject, can also introduce people to it for the first time. Don't limit your imagined audiences to those who already know about the subject. Ask yourself, "Who might learn something new from this information?"

A film on abortion rights brings up mixed feelings for most people. When I developed *The Fragile Promise of Choice*, about abortion rights in the U.S., I interviewed a wide spectrum of people who were being impacted by the increasing restrictions on women's health services. The stories in the film raise serious questions about the impact of limiting reproductive health services. And I try to give people the impetus to think "outside the box" and invite them to consider new ways of preventing unintended pregnancies, as well as considering a range of options that need to be protected when unintended pregnancies do occur.

When you can, invite those who may not agree with you to screenings. Recently I held a screening of the abortion series for a group of Catholic nuns who are educating themselves about a range of issues related to social justice. They truly appreciated the film, and lively non-judgmental discussion followed the screening!

To Support and Inspire

One of the gifts a documentary film can offer is to capture real-life situations so that the people in the film can see themselves anew. When we premiered *Why Do These Kids Love School?*, the audience was mainly teachers, parents, and children from the school.

After seeing the film, the community was amazed by what they'd just seen. They had never before stepped back that far to be able to watch the magic of what was happening throughout the school. Teachers and parents gave copies of the film to relatives (especially to grandparents of the students) and neighbors who didn't understand "alternative education." After the film was released on national PBS, teachers from across the country reported that they felt supported by the stories and examples in which they could see how alive progressive approaches make everybody feel!

To Activate

One of my goals is to both activate those who have not yet committed to action, and to support those who are already activists. Ask yourself, who do you think might be attracted to become more involved in the subject of your film? When we premiered *Fix-It Shops: An Endangered Species*, we invited a panel of local activists who used the film to get the word out to the community about a range of recycling opportunities. We provided literature with websites, e-mail addresses, and phone numbers.

We made it easy for the people who owned the Fix-It Shop to advertise the screening by giving them flyers to hand to customers.

SCREENING SIZES

You can hold a successful screening, of any size, no matter where you are or what your resources.

Small

Informal small screenings are the simplest to arrange. When you show your film in an informal way to a small group, the showing is generally free. The space can be your home or a friend's house or a small meeting room in a nearby community center. On a campus, screenings of six to twenty people work well in a dormitory lounge or a small classroom. You can contact guests on a one-to-one basis through a personal invitation by phone or e-mail.

Medium

For a medium-sized group (between twenty and seventy-five people), a good space might be a large home, library lecture room, community center, large classroom, clinic waiting room, church, or temple. Any organization that is supportive of the film might allow you to use a space in its facility. There might be a small fee. Publicity might be a small poster sent by e-mail, and posted in the area where the screening will be, if it is a public space. The fee might be an optional donation.

Large

If your plan is a large premiere, reserve the space well in advance. Larger premieres will require a theater, a high school auditorium, college lecture hall, or a large hotel conference space. Usually (but not always) there are expenses for larger spaces, and you will need to charge admission (unless you have donors to cover the costs).

My last three films had premieres of around one thousand people each. We had to reserve space at least six months in advance. One was in The Palace of Fine Arts, a theater within a museum; one was in The Fox Theater, in a converted Art Nouveau movie house; and the third was in a high school auditorium, run by the city, that holds 950 people. Another large venue was the shooting stage of a PBS station with whom I co-produced a film. In each case I had to "go shopping" to find the right choice, see spaces to get the right feel, juggle schedules to get the right date, negotiate to get the right price, etc. None of these were simple to put together, but all were worth the effort. One of the most effective springboards for launching any film is an eager audience of people who care about the subject and are eager to see whatever you have done. They take no convincing.

EXISTING AUDIENCES

There are a number of groups, places, and organizations which are natural to co-host a screening with you, groups who will invite their own circles, some of whom may even have spaces which are set up for screenings.

Interest Groups

Any community interested in your subject might have people who want to create a screening for or with you. When we were finishing the Ethiopian films, one of our interns was writing a thesis on Ethiopian women. She held a screening of *From Risk to Action* about women and AIDS in Ethiopia as part of her thesis presentation, inviting advisors, classmates, and her professors. These people came to the screening because the film met their hunger to learn more about what was happening in Ethiopia today, and also to learn more about their own interests in the subject of AIDS as it relates to Ethiopians in the United States.

Family, Friends, and Neighbors

The people you know, who have an investment in you personally, are the heart of outreach. Just as these people will be the first to give you money and honest feedback, they will be the first to come to your screenings, buy your film, and tell their friends. You can even have a smaller sneak preview with them, and they will help you spread the word for a larger screening.

Festivals

Entering and getting selected for a festival today is challenging. Because of the digital video revolution, entries to film festivals have increased significantly over the last decade. The competition is stiffer, and the pool of potential filmmakers is larger than ever before. But you can still enter and be shown in a film festival if you have a great film, and if you send your film to the right festival.

Every festival has its own preferences. Some festivals are strong in "cause" documentaries and others are strong in narrative fiction. Some want experimental works. Ideally, choose festivals or a division within a festival that offers you exposure to an audience that would be interested in using your film in the future.

If your film is accepted to a festival, and you decide to go, attend as many screenings of other filmmakers as possible. Have flyers or postcards and posters ready for people, so they know when to come to your screening and how to get in touch with you later. Even if your festival screening has a small attendance, don't be disheartened. One individual may be touched, and you will have planted a seed.

For one screening, I had only one person show up. After I got over the embarrassment, I held the screening (for one person). Afterward, we talked about the film. As a result, she became an intern. She donated the next year to working with me on what turned out to be a very popular poetry audiotape with original music called *Open Secret: The Poetry of Rumi*. These things *do* happen.

There is always a chance that a distributor at a festival will make an offer on the spot. It does happen — not as often as filmmakers hope it will, but it does. One of my interns, who went on to become a Hollywood producer, had her first feature film picked up at Sundance. So, I know for a fact from a firsthand report, it does happen!

A Few Places to Get Festival Information

Withoutabox (*www.withoutabox.com/*) is an international online exchange where you can submit your film to over 1600 festivals.

The Ultimate Film Festival Survival Guide by Chris Gore.

Wikipedia has a good section on film festivals (*www. en.wikipedia.org/wiki/Film_festival*).

College Campuses

College campuses are rewarding places to screen films. Students are curious, they tend to be open to new ideas, and they usually ask very thoughtful questions.

To Screen at a College Campus

1. Start locally. Begin by making a list of all the colleges in your area. Include universities, junior colleges, and special schools that focus on subjects that might be appropriate for your film.

2. See which ones have classes related to your subject. Teachers and professors are often looking for guest lecturers to add another dimension to what they are teaching.

3. Call or e-mail to ask if the person teaching would like to preview your work. You will need a good one-sheet project description, both to answer questions and to send to interested professors.

4. If they agree, send a VHS tape or DVD or put your film online so they can view it there. Two places to put your

film online are the Internet Archive (*www.archive.org*), and YouTube (*www.youtube.com*). (If you put your film online anywhere, make sure to read the site's copyright agreement before you post your film. Make sure you don't inadvertently give away rights by posting.)

5. Follow up with a phone call after they've had a chance to see the work. When you make your follow-up call, confirm that the film is appropriate for the class. If the answer is "yes," work out a time to schedule a showing.

When you hold a screening on a campus, try to be available afterwards. Students who want to make contact may feel shy in a larger group. Reach out to them and invite them to talk with you, so they will feel freer to initiate contact.

Conferences

Conferences can be a great place to screen your film, especially if you have a featured "plenary event" screening or a workshop. Films shown in the "video room" may be poorly attended when they compete with live sessions. If you are one of many films in a "side show" event, you will usually have to promote your screening yourself to get an audience.

People who attend a conference may come to one of these smaller screenings if the film is in their "field"; they appreciate a documentary on a subject that they care about. With effort and preparation, conferences can be a way to reach people likely to use your film in the future. Most conference sessions play simultaneously, back to back, except for the keynote addresses. People are often torn about which session to attend, and may not choose a film, which they know they can see later. Have plenty of materials to hand out for people who may not make it to the screening, but are interested.

To Screen at a Conference

- Find out which conferences address the subject(s) in your film. Use the Internet, and/or go to the library. Don't hesitate to make phone calls once you have a lead.

- Call the conference organizer and offer to show your film. If you have a strong film and describe it well, most conference organizers will consider a screening if they can fit it in. The organizer will usually need a six to nine-month lead time.

- Conference screenings range widely, from small breakaway sessions to a plenary with all attendees present. Make sure that you understand exactly where your film will be on the program.

There are no rules on payment. You may be paid to show your film. More often, you will be asked to show it for free. Sometimes you may need to pay a registration fee for the privilege of showing your film.

Meetings, Groups, and Organizations

For larger screenings and premieres, it is productive to collaborate with organizations in your geographical area. They might then help you contact other state and even national groups with local chapters. Whenever possible, find one person in each organization with whom you can communicate. See if you can work together to set up a screening or at least a preview. Again , your goal in setting up a screening is to find a good match between the place, the audience, and your work.

Seminars and Workshops

Are there skills or approaches you feel that you want to teach? If you have an interest in working with individual film students or simply those interested in filmmaking, you might plan to hold a seminar or workshop at which you show excerpts of your films. Additional activities can include lectures by you on aspects of filmmaking. As a follow-up, offer a variety of handouts that go deeper into a subject than you can speak about in a single day. There should always be time for students to share their own interests and concerns. These events work well for one full day on a Saturday or Sunday. Fees can range from $25 to more than $100 depending on the setting.

VIRTUAL AUDIENCES

The Internet

One of the most potentially productive venues for a film, as a resource for both audiences and screenings, is the Internet.

We just received a generous foundation grant to put the distilled essence (twenty-seven minutes of the two-and-a-half hour set) of the trilogy of Motherhood by Choice up on YouTube and seventeen other Internet sites.

YouTube (*www.youtube.com*), now one of the most popular Internet video sites, began a couple of years ago. Suddenly, with this free venue, it has become easy for anyone to post a video online. Within months, millions of clips of everything from skateboarding to the Daily Show appeared on the Internet. Now anyone can become a "movie star" or a producer. You can too.

Wikipedia has a good comparison chart showing dozens of online video hosts at *www.en.wikipedia.org/wiki/Comparison_ of_video_services*.

Again, if you post your movie on any site, make sure you read the current copyright rules before you post. Make sure you aren't giving away any rights to the site, or their parent company.

Use keywords to help people search for your films

When you post your film online, most sites have a form that asks for "keywords" to describe your film. You can make it easier for people to find your film by using as many related keywords as possible.

Publish-on-demand services on the Internet make it easy for anyone to publish and distribute a DVD online.

One of the easier to use publish-on-demand publishers is Lulu.com (*www.lulu.com*). Lulu.com's strength is its simplicity. Upload your DVD and cover art and approve the result, and the site will give you a unique lulu.com web address for your DVD. Anyone can then buy your DVD online. Lulu handles everything: printing, mailing and collecting money, and sending you royalties. You can set the royalty amount on each DVD.

CustomFlix (*www.customflix.com*) is an excellent print-on-demand DVD publisher. CustomFlix has a history of working successfully with independent filmmakers, and they seem to be constantly improving and expanding their film distribution options.

Where to Download the Films

You can see or download most of my films online, for free, at the Internet Archive: *www.archive.org/search.php?query=fadiman*.

The Internet Archive is a constantly expanding digital library of Internet sites and other cultural artifacts in digital form. Like a paper library, the Internet Archive provides free access to researchers, historians, scholars, and the general public.

Motherhood by Choice is a good example of the process that a film goes through for Internet distribution. We sent a DVD master to AVGeeks at *www.avgeeks.com*. They digitized the film and encoded it in several formats: MPEG-4 for high definition; MPEG-2 for DVD quality; and two streaming formats, one for high-speed connections, and one for dial-up. Because we wanted public access television stations to be able to produce their own DVDs, we asked AVGeeks to create a disk image of the film that stations could download and burn to DVD. A disk image is a complete digital copy of a finished DVD. The station can get a finished DVD by merely downloading the image and writing it to a blank DVD.

You do not receive any income directly from online distribution through the Internet Archive. Your income, if any, comes from grants from non-profit organizations who may choose to fund this distribution. You also get publicity for your film, and people can click through to your site. What you are doing is making contact with people who might be interested in supporting future work.

Public and Community Access TV

We offered *Motherhood by Choice* to every public access television station in the country. This is an affordable way to get national exposure for your films.

If you decide to screen on public access television, start in your own community. Find your public access station by looking in the phone book, or by using the Internet.

Global Village CAT has links to 700 public or community access television sites: *http://www.communitymedia.se/cat/linksus.htm*.

After you find your local public access station, call them and ask if they will broadcast your program.

You can also screen your film on public access television stations outside your local area. Work outward in concentric circles, contacting stations in communities near yours. Most stations require that someone from within the community bring or send them the film.

If you have a good, mutually supportive relationship with a national organization or group, you can ask that they work with you to reach out to their members nationwide and find people who will hand-deliver your film to their local public access stations.

Whatever the subject of your film, there are usually national organizations who would be interested in helping you if you do the groundwork. You may still have to make the contact with the local stations and then make the connection with someone in the local group. Generally, the organizations don't have enough staff to do it for you.

To Screen Your Film on Public Access Television

1. Find your local public access television station. It is probably listed on one of these sites:

   Alliance for Community Media *www.alliancecm.org/*

   The Global Village CAT *www.openchannel.se/cat* or *www. communitymedia.se/cat/linksus.htm*

2. Call the public access station and ask for instructions on how to submit your film.

3. Send or arrange delivery of a copy of your film in the format required by the station. The most common formats are VHS, SVHS, DV, and DVCAM.

4. For public access television stations outside your local area find someone in each community to sponsor the film and deliver it to the station. (Even if you have a local sponsor, contact the station yourself to make sure the film will be screened.)

PBS

My experience is that your best chance of getting your film broadcast on PBS is to start by co-producing with and/or submitting your film to your local PBS station for broadcast. Getting a film on national PBS is a competitive, labor-intensive, and time-consuming process.

If your subject matter is controversial, there are only a few slots in national programming such as *Point of View* at *www .pov.org*.

In the past, I have worked through local stations first. Then, if the film goes to national, the local station deals directly with national PBS.

The "PBS Producer's Handbook" at *www.aptvs.org/aptweb. nsf/vProducers/Index-Producers* describes PBS requirements in detail.

THE BUSINESS OF SCREENINGS

For many kinds of screenings such as conferences, festivals, informal house parties, etc. you do not generally charge admission. In the past, filmmakers might rent their 16mm films to be shown to schools and churches, but now, with low-priced DVDs readily available, 16mm film rentals are rare.

The question is: Where and when do you charge?

There are times when it is appropriate to charge admission or ask for a fee such as when you provide a screening at which you will speak. Also, you will charge admission when people come to see your film in a theater. What is appropriate is different in every case.

Questions to consider when deciding whether or not to charge admission to a screening:

1. Which population? Generally, you look at the financial situation of a particular group, and base your decision on their ability to pay. I would never charge admission for a screening in Ethiopia, given the extreme poverty, nor for a screening at a women's clinic that serves low-income

patients. But, if I hold a screening at a well-funded private school, it may be very appropriate to charge for tickets or request a fee. When I hold a premiere, I often use a sliding scale, so that people on low incomes pay very little and those with resources pay more.

2. Does the event have a co-sponsor? If an organization is sponsoring your screening with you, you can negotiate with them to see what the fee for admission should be. A co-sponsor will often share in the expenses, share the profits of the event, and act as a financial conduit for you. They may also give you use of their database for a mailing (or e-mailing) or provide guest speakers.

Five Different Ways to Approach Admission and Fundraising at Screenings

1. Free: no entry price and no request for funds after the screening.

2. Free, with a request for donations afterward: You don't charge an entry fee, but you do ask for funds after the screening. Tell people beforehand that funds will be solicited at the screening. Usually you hand out donation envelopes with your address on them, and pass a basket after the screening.

3. Sliding scale admission: The lowest figure may be free, and then include the opportunity for generous donations.

4. General Admission: Plan to charge approximately the going theatrical rate in your area. Find out what theaters are charging and be in that range.

5. Fundraiser: Set a higher ticket price for "suggested donations." Beginning tickets might begin at $25, with the option of $500 or $1,000 or more tax-deductible contributions.

REACHING PEOPLE THROUGH SCREENINGS

Lynn Adams, the co-founder of Pyramid Media, took my first film *Radiance* into distribution. She once said, "The best way to create a market for your film, is to first give it away."

She told me that in 1978, and it is still true today. The reason it's true is because the beginning filmmaker's enemy is anonymity. By giving your film away, you get your film in front of people, where hopefully it will generate word-of-mouth publicity.

Pyramid took two of my early films, *Radiance* and *Why Do These Kids Love School?* We gave them away to key users at schools, colleges, universities, and others. The resulting word-of-mouth publicity helped both of these films become best sellers!

In addition to your desire to have audiences see the film, you want them to remember the film, and you. People will connect you, the filmmaker, with the film more than you may realize.

When you speak, include anecdotes about the making of the movie. Audiences love to hear real-life details. When possible, after a screening, you want to create an atmosphere that is supportive, collegial, and allows for open discussion.

Every time you screen your film, plant seeds for the future. Be sure to bring materials with you: flyers about the film; notices for future screenings; cards to hand out so audiences can find you; and sign-up sheets for your database.

KEY POINTS

꘡ After the exhaustion of production, screenings will restore your energy!

꘡ A screening is an ideal way to publicize your film and make new contacts.

꘡ Your goals in setting up a screening are to find a good match between the place, the audience, and your film.

꘡ One of the most powerful springboards for launching any film is ready-made audiences who already are interested in the subject.

꘡ One option to get started is to broadcast through your local public access television station.

꘡ The Internet is an outstanding resource for distribution. Don't overlook it. The possibilities for filmmakers are expanding and changing daily.

꘡ The best way to sell a film may be to give it away and generate word-of-mouth publicity.

CHAPTER 20

PUBLICITY

1. *The approaches described in this chapter are ones which I've tested and found to work.*

2. *No matter how many people help you, you will be the one responsible for getting the word out about your film.*

3. *The most effective energy for successful publicity is personal contact.*

4. *Screenings themselves are excellent publicity, and a great way to make personal contact with people interested in you and your film.*

5. *Publicizing a film can be at least as demanding as making a film.*

Once you survive the process of making and finishing a film, another level of work now begins: Getting the word out!

While many people can help you publicize your film, the job of organizing this effort and planning how you want to do it is yours.

Without publicity, even good films disappear from view. Making sure that films are promoted, shown, and distributed is as important as making them. With or without a distributor, the best gift you can give yourself as a filmmaker is to continue to make sure people hear about your work and that they have chances to see it.

We held a gala premiere for *Woman by Woman: New Hope for the Villages of India,* in the city where I live. As I stood outside the theater that evening, I could see a line of ticket holders stretching around the block.

We were sold out. Almost a thousand people!

Inside the lobby, chefs were serving donated hors d'oeuvres from gourmet Indian restaurants to the reception guests: funders, local officials, visitors from India, and the press.

Inside my head, a cascade of three solid months of publicity continued to tumble around — articles, flyers, handbills, posters, and e-mails to friends, colleagues, and the Indian community throughout the Bay Area.

Even though my team and I had worked tirelessly to create a film with integrity, there would have been no one standing outside the theater if we hadn't done the publicity, outreach, and promotion in the months leading up to the screening.

The publicity tools and techniques that follow are practical approaches I've tested and found to work over the last thirty years. These techniques are what we use to fill theaters.

Materials to Distribute

Once you set a screening date, make sure you know how much of the publicity will be up to you. If it is your event with no co-hosts, then responsibility is yours. If it is co-sponsored, everything should be shared, so make sure you find out how the publicity will be divided. Once you know what share is yours, your work begins immediately. Sometimes the other party is not able to produce what they intended or promised, so do not take anything for granted.

Ways to Get the Word Out

- Tell people about the screening, and ask them to tell their friends. Word of mouth is *the* best publicity!

- Make telephone calls to groups and interested individuals. Create a telephone tree.

- Send out "Save the Date" e-mails to everyone on your lists. Ask your connections to then send it on to their lists.

- Announce the screening in newsletters of interested organizations.

- Send postcards to your own and other mailing lists.

- Distribute and post informational flyers.

- Post the name, time, and place of the screening on relevant websites.

- Let the local press know about the screenings.

- Be pro-active and offer to be interviewed by the press.

- Contact community colleges, universities, student groups, and other community organizations to let the right teachers and organizational leaders know. Note: Photos fax poorly. If you fax, use graphics without photos.

Flyers and Posters

The goal of a flyer or a poster is to catch someone's eye. Make your design bold and simple. Look at bulletin boards, see what catches your eye, and let that inspire you!

When you finish your posters/flyers, put them up everywhere you can think of, including campuses, coffeehouses, and libraries. In some communities there are services that post your flyers for a fee.

Handbills and Postcards

A handbill or postcard should be easy to pick up and hard to lose. You can print them inexpensively, four on a page with black ink on colored cardstock. Four-color postcards are also affordable when purchased in bulk over the Internet.

Put postcards and quarter-page handouts in places where people who you hope will come to your screening go, such as bookstores, meetings of interest groups, film department classes, etc. Whenever you send something by mail — a letter or an invoice or a payment — add a postcard or handbill to the envelope.

Handouts at Screenings

Good publicity sets a chain of connections into motion. Be prepared to give everyone who attends a screening something to take home. Plan to create handouts that will inform audience members so that they can continue to use your film and the ideas in it. This is also an opportunity to publicize related activities and resources in your community and beyond.

Kinds of materials attendees might appreciate include:

- Information about how to order your film
- Names and full contact information from organizations in the community
- Names of guest speakers from the community who could present at other events
- Internet sites about the subject of your film and related national organizations
- Related books and related films
- Pamphlets and flyers printed by groups with an interest in your subject

WORKING WITH THE MEDIA

Your goal in working with the media is to promote your project in print, from a mention in a calendar section to a front-page article. Calendar listings are straightforward. Simply follow the publication's rules and meet its deadline. Getting an article published is more labor intensive.

First, you need to approach your local news media, and find a reporter who is interested. Be prepared to "pitch" a story about your film and its potential impact.

To create this "pitch," write a brief description of your film and the reasons why people would want to watch it. The "pitch" should include points from the original one-sheet concept statement that you wrote when you were doing initial research. (See Chapter 2, Focusing Your Energies, for instructions on preparing a one-sheet.)

If the project has continued to evolve, include new points, and your most recent insights and findings.

Invite people you trust to read the "pitch," and get their opinions. Being objective about your own work may be hard. Most friends will be glad to help you craft it. Your goal in writing a pitch is to describe one or more "hooks" that will compel someone to write about the film. When we premiered *Fix-It Shops* we got five feature articles including a front-page story and a four-color center spread. The "hook" was that this film was about a local business that provided a direct service to the same community served by those five papers.

Finding local radio and television opportunities involves the same basic process. Make your pitch with the goal of finding out who would be interested in your subject and focus on reaching those individuals. In all of these "approaches," you will need a press kit.

Press Kits

The goal of a press kit is to impress a reporter, editor, or talk show producer at a glance. They might want to read more, but they should be able to skim what you've put together and "get it" immediately. A good press kit has some bold, eye-catching messages, as well as factual material in an attractive presentation that makes it easy for a reporter to write about you, your project, or an event.

What Goes into a Press Kit

A good press kit will contain some or all of these items:

- A press release (one-page description of the film)
- Brief biographies of key people on the team
- Any past articles about the film
- Quotes from people who've seen the film
- Good contact information including current phone numbers and e-mail addresses
- Photographs or other images

Press Releases

A major step toward getting an article published is a good press release, which may come in your press kit or be sent separately. A press release is a tool to communicate the newsworthiness of an issue in a matter of seconds. Press releases generally provide background for a story or interview. It should include specific details on the time and place of the activity, a few lines of background on the event or issue, and a quote by the group's spokesperson when applicable. Where to start? Begin by writing a one-page summary of an angle that will appeal to the community you are trying to reach. Include the most essential information in the first paragraph. Press releases should be double-spaced and no more than one page in length.

Add a short cover letter (less than a page) with your personal touch. If you have a DVD available, put one in the package too.

Test, Test, Test Your DVD!

Before sending out a DVD, test it on more than one DVD player. Some DVDs will play on some computers, not others, and not on certain off-the-shelf DVD players.

Send the press release and cover letter to the reporter.

In a few days, follow up with a phone call.

Media Advisories

Sometimes you will want to send a "Media Advisory" instead of a Press Release. What is the difference between them? A Media Advisory usually outlines the schedule or details of a time-sensitive event you or your group are involved in or hosting with information about the event's "who, what, when, where, and why" and not much more.

Like the press release, it should be no more than one page. Send your media advisory out about two weeks in advance of your event. A few days before the event, follow up the advisory with a phone call.

If a reporter is coming to a screening, tell your team that the media has been invited and suggest that they have some key messages in mind before speaking to reporters.

Personal Contact

Publicity is ultimately about personal contact.

Getting your work promoted and seen is a process of continually communicating with people and capturing their interest. If you are appearing before a class, your audience is guaranteed. But if you are having a small screening open to the public at a local library, you need to make contacts and get the word out more than once.

You will need to meet or talk on the phone to reporters and others. This is no time to be shy. Call your local newspaper, radio, and TV stations and find out who covers the issues described in your film.

When you have the name of the right person, follow up with a phone call.

If the journalist or reporter asks to see a preview copy, send it the same day or even hand deliver it if you can. One week after you put something in the-mail for review, call to verify that the tape or DVD arrived. Things get lost in the newsroom, and a polite call to jog the reporter's memory is not inappropriate.

SCREENINGS FOR PUBLICITY

The goal of all publicity is to reach the right people, and to reach as many of them as possible. One of the most effective ways to reach people is to be present at the screenings. Screenings create opportunities for new people to see the film and meet the filmmaker. During discussion afterwards, as people share their views, they feel connected to you and to your film. People who feel "connected" in this way will tell others to see the film. This is publicity that money can't buy.

Motherhood by Choice recently worked its way through this system as a result of both effort and synchronicity. I was invited to show the work-in-progress of the film to the local chapter of Medical Students for Choice. The day of the screening, we had a great turnout of staff and students from Stanford's Medical School.

After the screening, a student asked if I could do a screening at the Medical Students for Choice regional conference. I said "yes." We prepared an inviting handout, and had an overflow turnout at the conference screening. Following the screening, I attended an informal lunch, hoping to network further.

There, I met the CEO of Planned Parenthood of California. She had seen the impact the film had on the students. With her leadership, plans were soon underway for us to screen the film in Washington, D.C. at the National March for Women's Lives.

Within a few months following the D.C. showing, we were selling copies of the film, by the hundreds, to groups across the country. Everything had begun with one local screening, which I attended and where I met someone who took the film to the next level.

Publicity works best when you are willing to put yourself forward. Your willingness to do the work described in this chapter will enable you to reach the audiences you envision for your film.

KEY POINTS

- The easiest place to do publicity is within your own community for a local screening.

- Keep these basic resources in mind for all screenings:
  - flyer
  - handbill or postcard
  - press kit
  - press release

- Publicity is ultimately about personal contact. For greatest success, you will need to meet and talk to the people you want to reach. If not in person, then by phone.

- Let everyone you talk with know about your event and about your film. You are your own best press agent.

CHAPTER 21

REACHING POTENTIAL VIEWERS: DISTRIBUTION

1. *Once you've finished your film, the question is "What distribution plan meets your real needs?"*

2. *Options for distribution include: self, commercial, and combined.*

3. *The Internet makes self-distribution a viable choice for anyone.*

4. *Before signing with any distributor, do your due diligence. Find out about their catalog, their general reputation in the film community and with individual filmmakers.*

5. *Don't sign a contract without first showing it to someone familiar with such contracts. Be sure you understand what you are signing.*

THE OPTIONS

There are three general types of distribution:

- With a commercial distributor

- Self-distribution

- A combination of self, commercial and "other." This hybrid approach is becoming popular, particularly as the Internet opens new doors. The question for you as a filmmaker is: "What meets your real needs?"

Self-distribution has several advantages, including more control as to when, where, and to whom your film is shown and sold. And there may be more profits for you. The disadvantages are that self-distribution may be expensive up front, time-consuming, and not easy to walk away from and "take a break." You, or someone, needs to continue to fulfill sales and reach customers, even when you are traveling or busy with other projects.

The advantages to using a distributor can be substantial. They can usually reach markets that may be difficult for you to locate and penetrate. However, because those sales come in through another door, not yours, you might lose contact with those who buy and use your films. And you'll make a much smaller percentage of profit on each sale.

I prefer to do both, if I can. Ideally, I find a distributor who is a good match, and I retain the right in the contract to do some self-distribution. I find this approach both profitable and rewarding.

We recently sold thousands of DVDs through self-distribution. We began by taking a road trip through California down Interstate 99 with screenings at fourteen planned stops along the way, adding more as we traveled. Four of us packed into a motor home with supplies for a two-week journey. We set off. On our journey, we showed the DVD in living rooms, on college campuses, in churches, clinics, government offices, libraries, and a union hall packed with activists.

Wherever we went, we sold DVDs (the self-distribution part). When people asked, "Where can we buy a VHS video tape?" we sent them to our website, which had prices and our distributor's contact information. Sometimes people ordered a hundred DVDs. We sent their order to our office to fill.

After the success of the California road trip, and after reviewing what we learned, we scheduled a national trip with stops in dozens of cities and ended up selling more than forty thousand DVDs.

PROFESSIONAL DISTRIBUTION

From the outside, commercial distribution seems to offer a panacea. The myth goes something like this: You finish your film, give it to a distributor, and the royalty checks start rolling in, providing you with enough money to fund your next project. Word gets out and funders start coming to you to ask if they can donate money or invest in your work.

Does it actually happen that way?

Rarely.

For most of us, it's more like this. First, you go shopping to locate the right potential distributor, who then previews your film. If you find a good match, you then work out a deal. If you agree, and the distributor acquires the film, the challenge of doing promotion begins for both of you.

A Few Places to Find Names of Distributors

Finding the names and addresses of distributors requires some research. Here are links to helpful books and websites:

The Media Research Center at University of California - Berkeley: *www.lib.berkeley.edu/MRC/Distributors.html*

CustomFlix: *www.customflix.com*. Read Mark Bosko's "Top Ten Tips to Film Distribution" in the Distribution How-To section of the CustomFlix website.

The Complete Independent Movie Marketing Handbook by Mark Steven Bosko (*www.mwp.com*)

The *Independent Film & Videomaker's Guide* by Michael Wiese (*www.mwp.com*)

Finding a Distributor

When it goes well, the advantages of using a distributor can be considerable. Ideally, the distribution company creates a promotional program for you with support materials for specific audiences.

The Advantages of Finding a Distributor

What distributors may do for you:

- Put a listing with a description of your film in their catalog
- Handle all inquiries and orders that come to them
- Make sure that payments for sales are received
- Use their existing mailing list to reach customers who are familiar with their work
- Reach universities and other organizations that prefer to work with distributors rather than independent filmmakers
- Get a UPC (Universal Product Code) bar code for the package, so the tape or DVD can be scanned at the point of sale
- Send you royalty checks.
- Market your film through their "business to business" relationships

Sometimes (but not always) a distributor will also:

- Package your tape nicely
- Produce a special brochure for your film
- Send out a special mailing with your film and similar films
- Submit your film to festivals
- Advise you where to show your film

The reality is that it may be difficult for first-time filmmakers to find the right distributor at first. Some distributors prefer filmmakers with track records. After you have produced a successful film, you will have a better chance of getting a distributor. Often, the same distributor who takes one of your films will want to continue to carry your work and build a following for you.

People who do break into the industry with first films generally have this in common: *They made a great film.* The single best thing you can do to increase your chances of finding a distributor is to make the best possible film you can.

Another way you can connect with distributors is to show your film at festivals. Well-known, well-attended festivals like Sundance, Toronto, Berlin, or Cannes get thousands of entries each year, so you will need an exceptional film to be selected. There are hundreds of other smaller festivals for which your film may be perfect.

It can be done! Each of the filmmakers in all of those festivals started out just like you, with a vision. Film by film, festival by festival, connection by connection, they worked their way up. (See Chapter 19 for sources of information on film festivals.)

Evaluating a Distributor

Before you deal with a distribution company, check their catalogue and get in touch with one or more filmmakers they represent. It is difficult to evaluate distributors unless you talk to experienced filmmakers with films in distribution and others associated with filmmaking who know who is reputable. If you are new to this world, it's hard to know what or who to believe.

When you look at a distributor's catalog, figure out which films have been released in the past few years. Contact the producers of these films, and ask them about their experiences with that distributor. Ask if their films were promoted well, if the distributor paid on time, and whether the distributor honored the terms of the contract.

Every distributor you talk to will have one question in mind above all, "Will your film sell to my market?"

Distributors need films to fill their particular market niche. They will take your film only if it fits in their catalog, and if they believe they can sell it to their clientele. Hopefully, if finding a distributor is your goal, you will find a distributor who is a good match for you and for your film.

Signing with a Distributor

The First Step: The Deal Memo

If a distributor likes your film, you will be presented with an offer, usually in a deal memo. Before you sign anything, show the deal memo to a lawyer or to several filmmakers with films in distribution.

A lawyer will explain what the wording of the deal memo really means. There are a number of different distribution rights. The distributor will try to acquire as many as possible, and you may want to keep as many as possible.

This is a complex area, and you have to be aware of what you are giving up, and what you want to retain. Among other things, you may be obligating yourself to a deal for five or more years. Read carefully what, if any, escape clause there is.

Only when you understand the details should you begin to negotiate with the distributor.

The Second Step: The Detailed Contract

When you reach agreement on a deal, the distributor prepares a detailed contract. The detailed contract is where you really have to be careful. Once you sign it, you are obligated to everything in it, including the fine print.

Before You Sign Anything!

Show the detailed contract to someone (a lawyer or another filmmaker) who has experience in this area.

Go over the contract and clarify each item, until you work out the fairest contract possible. When you sign a contract, try to retain as many rights as possible, which you may want for another deal down the road. In many cases, you will want a different distributor for certain other rights.

Some of the Distribution Rights That May Be on the Table

- Theatrical

- Foreign

- Home video or DVD

- Broadcast television

- Video to universities and industry

When a Distributor Acquires Your Film

After a distributor takes a film, you will need to provide certain materials to support the distributor's promotional efforts.

For a larger campaign, a distributor might create one or more of these: press kits; posters; flyers; logos; trailers; and other marketing materials. Give the distributor bios, images, articles, and other materials describing you and the film.

The distributor then makes your film available to all the markets specified in the distribution contract. Most distributors produce a catalog, and your film will be listed in that catalog. The distributor usually has a website, and your film will be listed on that site.

The distributor will set prices and people will contact the distributor to ask for your film. The percentage of the purchase price that you receive varies widely, anywhere from 8% to 70%

depending on the contract and specifics such as whether they do the duplication, or you do.

Stories from the Trenches

People's experiences with distributors vary widely. Here are two tales from my own encounters, one positive and one negative.

First, a positive story, about what happened during the final days of editing *When Abortion Was Illegal*.

It was early evening, the end of a long day of editing, when I got a phone call from a distributor, Mitchell Block of Direct Cinema Limited.

He said, "I heard you were making a film about abortion rights. I was in the neighborhood and wanted to see what you are doing."

He came over to where we were working, viewed the cut, and ordered take-out Chinese food for my team. While we were eating dinner, he offered to distribute the film.

I accepted his offer. Soon afterwards, I was on vacation, regaining my strength after months of intensive editing. I was in a hammock in Hawaii, when one of my children handed me the phone. It was Mitchell, encouraging me to make a 16mm film print and enter my documentary into the Academy Award short film competition.

Having no idea what I was getting into, I agreed. Over the next few weeks, I spent thousands of dollars making a film print. A few months later, I got a call telling me that *When Abortion Was Illegal* was nominated for the Oscar. He had an intuition, and he was right. That was the happy story.

The other story is a sad one. Early in my career, I made a short film called *World Peace Is a Local Issue*, about citizens who had stepped forward to ask their local government to support a nuclear freeze resolution. After the film was finished, I sent a mass mailing, offering the film to peace groups and activists for $19.95.

I got eighty requests for purchase of the film from groups and individuals willing to take it sight unseen. I was overwhelmed by these requests, and wasn't yet set up to serve all those people. So I signed with a distributor who said he would handle everything, and took over all rights. The distributor immediately contacted all those same people and told them the film would now cost close to $200.

Not only did every request die on the vine, but also he never returned the leads to me. I was so inexperienced, and foolish, that I had not even kept copies of those names and addresses. Signing with that distributor was a huge mistake. And I should have kept the right to serve the "home market" myself and let him take universities and libraries. Never again have I made a deal with a distributor where I did not reserve some rights to home video sales.

SELF-DISTRIBUTION

Despite the myth that an artist should be free to focus on making art and leave business matters — like distribution — to others, the reality is that as a filmmaker you will probably have to get involved in distribution. In fact, you should want to wear the distribution hat at least some of the time, in order to get your film out in the world.

The day you start a film is not too soon to begin thinking about who is going to see it, who is going to show it, and how it's going to be used. Budget for that step. When fundraising, it is easy to neglect distribution costs in the budget. The eventual expense of launching your film — in both time and money — may be invisible at first, because that stage seems so far away. But as you look to the future, consider the possibility that you might self-distribute. People do it all the time. Some out of choice, some out of necessity.

Self-distribution means learning about marketing, running a small business, and usually putting aside the "creative" side of filmmaking for a while in order to become a salesperson who also needs to fill orders!

My own experience with self-distribution is that it is barely worth the time, cost, and hassle. But I have done it for years, still do it, and plan to continue, even though it is hard work!

After trying a variety of different distribution approaches, I am actually doing a hybrid.

In addition to self-distribution, and having nine films with distributors, I am also putting all of my films on the Internet, so that they can be previewed by anyone. Most can also be downloaded. I have needed to negotiate with my distributors to allow people to download certain films.

I tell distributors that while they may lose a few sales when people download the films from the Internet, they will gain new sales when people are able to preview them.

Bottom line, even with all the challenges, there are substantial benefits to self-distribution. You get to know your customers personally, you control how much you charge, with whom you do outreach, and promoting the film your way. You also have the freedom to sell films at a low cost and, when it feels right, give them away.

A Few Ways to Use the Internet to Self-Distribute

Set up a website, and let people buy films using PayPal (*www. paypal.com*). The PayPal site explains how you can use PayPal Merchant Tools to receive payments for your film.

Lulu.com (*www.lulu.com*) will publish and distribute your DVD as a DVD-on-Demand.

CustomFlix (*www.customflix.com*) will publish and distribute your DVD as a DVD-on-Demand.

Benefits of Self-Distribution

- You make a greater profit on each sale
- You have the freedom to sell to whomever you wish
- You can finalize your own graphics
- You can set up your own website and sell films on it
- You have more control

STUDY GUIDES

Study guides may be tedious to produce, but are a potentially valuable endeavor. Many educators want study guides when they are considering purchase of a film for teaching purposes.

Many instructors prefer educational films that are around twenty minutes long. This gives the instructors time to show the film in class and hold a discussion afterwards. A study guide supplements the classroom discussions and makes it easy for the professor to give homework assignments.

If you decide to write a study guide, review existing ones that accompany films similar to yours. This will give you an idea of the layout, style, and language that the educational market prefers.

OUTREACH

The real reward of all forms of outreach (screenings, Internet listing, working with a distributor, etc.) is getting your film out in the world. All of these efforts help you get a message, about which you are passionate, out in the world.

One of the key messages of this book is that the responsibility of getting your film out in the world is yours and yours alone. No one else will do it for you the way you can do it for yourself.

Your job, after making the film, is to connect with audiences who can then see it and use it.

KEY POINTS

🍂 Categories of distribution: professional distribution; self-distribution; and (what most filmmakers end up doing) a combination of these.

🍂 The question to ask yourself about distribution is "What meets my real needs?"

🍂 As a filmmaker, you will probably have to wear the distribution hat some of the time if you want to get your film out into the world.

🍂 When fundraising, don't forget to add distribution costs into your budget.

🍂 Before you sign with a distributor, do your homework.

CONCLUSION

We have come to the end of this book and it's time to reflect and to act. You and I have films to make.

My current film, *Stealing America: Vote by Vote,* is omnipresent for me now, fourteen hours a day.

You may already have an idea for a film of your own, an idea that ignites passion in you. Or you may just have a sense of something that "might" turn into a film, but you don't know what to do next.

Not knowing where to start is very common, and all filmmakers experience it.

The solution is just to begin, whether it's writing down your ideas, or finding a camera and shooting something — anything — to get started.

There's an old saying, and it goes like this: Go simple; go small; go now!

If the prospect of "making a movie" is overwhelming, make your first film small, no more than five minutes. Ideally, focus on something local: the places, people, and things in your own life.

Just pick up a pad and start writing.

Or pick up a camera — any camera — and shoot some footage. You might interview someone you find interesting, or you might document a project or a place or even an object that intrigues you. When you have ten or twelve minutes of footage, stop shooting.

Edit your twelve minutes down to five, give it a title, and post the finished product on YouTube or another Internet video site. Then, make another five-minute film, and another after that.

If your films reflect your own passion, chances are they will inspire passion in others, and soon you will have an audience.

Eventually, as your film projects get larger, you will work with others to bring them into being. Your job then will be to choose the people with whom you want to work, figure out how to raise money for the film, and then manage to keep the whole project on course.

It will also be your job to tell the truth to yourself and the others as you work together, even if the truth is painful.

When the film is finished, your job will then be to make sure people see it and use it.

You have before you the opportunity of a lifetime: a chance to create a film that reflects what you've lived through, what you've learned, what you've gained and what you've lost. Filmmaking sometimes feels like a burden, but mostly it will keep you meaningfully busy. Then one day, when the end is in sight, you realize that the genuine satisfaction of having finished a film is well worth the effort.

My blessings to you, and my most genuine wishes for success.

Good luck!

ABOUT THE AUTHORS

Dorothy Fadiman, Documentary Filmmaker

Dorothy has been producing award-winning media with a focus on social justice and human rights since 1976. She lives in Menlo Park, California, where she moved to pursue graduate work in communication studies at Stanford University.

Subjects range from the light of Spirit in every faith (*Radiance: The Experience of Light*) to progressive education that honors children's natural knowing (*Why Do These Kids Love School?*) to the extraordinary healing journey of a woman with spinal cord injury (*Moment by Moment: The Healing Journey of Molly Hale*). Her interest in women's issues includes these films: *Woman by Woman: New Hope for the Villages of India*; a three-film series, *From the Back Alleys to the Supreme Court & Beyond*; and *From Risk to Action: Women and HIV/AIDS in Ethiopia*, one of a five-film series *Seeds of Hope: Meeting the Challenges of HIV/AIDS in Ethiopia*. Her films have been shown on PBS stations nationwide, plus a number of international venues.

Her current projects include a documentary exploring a spectrum of "irregularities" in the 2004 Presidential election and another on the disenfranchisement of Native American voters.

Among her honors are an Academy Award nomination, an Emmy, the Gold Medal from the Corporation for Public Broadcasting, and more than fifty other film awards.

In addition to producing documentary films, Dorothy teaches, gives seminars, leads workshops, and trains interns in filmmaking.

Dorothy's website is *www.concentric.org*. Her e-mail is *info@concentric.org*.

Photo by Dennis Tyler

Tony Levelle

Inspired by such available-light and low-budget films as Robert Rodriguez's *El Mariachi* and Jon Jost's *Frameup*, filmmaker Tony Levelle set out on a mission to learn how to do the same.

He had the good fortune to attend a seminar by Dorothy Fadiman, who not only finished all the films she started and got every film into distribution, but kept them there!

He eventually worked with Fadiman, and his new co-authored book — *Producing with Passion: Making Films That Change the World* — is the result of their collaboration to share these techniques with others.

The quality of this book so impressed the publisher that even before it was finished they signed Tony to solo author a second book titled *Digital Video Secrets: What the Pros Know and The Manuals Don't Tell You*, which will be released in Fall 2008.

Tony exemplifies the qualities all filmmakers need to survive: passion, persistence and vision.

For more information about *Producing With Passion* go to www.producingwithpassion.com.

INDEX

FILM DIRECTING: SHOT BY SHOT
VISUALIZING FROM CONCEPT TO SCREEN

STEVEN D. KATZ

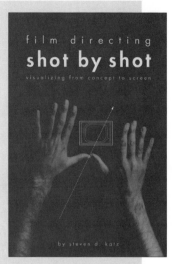

BEST SELLER
OVER 190,000 COPIES SOLD!

Film Directing: Shot by Shot — with its famous blue cover — is the best-known book on directing and a favorite of professional directors as an on-set quick reference guide.

This international bestseller is a complete catalog of visual techniques and their stylistic implications, enabling working filmmakers to expand their knowledge.

Contains in-depth information on shot composition, staging sequences, visualization tools, framing and composition techniques, camera movement, blocking tracking shots, script analysis, and much more.

Includes over 750 storyboards and illustrations, with never-before-published storyboards from Steven Spielberg's *Empire of the Sun*, Orson Welles' *Citizen Kane*, and Alfred Hitchcock's *The Birds*.

"(To become a director) you have to teach yourself what makes movies good and what makes them bad. John Singleton has been my mentor... he's the one who told me what movies to watch and to read Shot by Shot.*"*
> – Ice Cube, *New York Times*

"A generous number of photos and superb illustrations accompany each concept, many of the graphics being from Katz' own pen... Film Directing: Shot by Shot *is a feast for the eyes."*
> – *Videomaker* Magazine

"... demonstrates the visual techniques of filmmaking by defining the process whereby the director converts storyboards into photographed scenes."
> – *Back Stage Shoot*

"Contains an encyclopedic wealth of information."
> – *Millimeter* Magazine

STEVEN D. KATZ is also the author of *Film Directing: Cinematic Motion*.

$27.95 · 366 PAGES · ORDER NUMBER 7RLS · ISBN: 0-941188-10-8

FILM & VIDEO BOOKS

Archetypes for Writers: *Using the Power of Your Subconscious*
Jennifer Van Bergen / $22.95

Art of Film Funding, The: *Alternate Financing Concepts*
Carole lee Dean / $26.95

Cinematic Storytelling: *The 100 Most Powerful Film Conventions Every Filmmaker Must Know* / Jennifer Van Sijll / $24.95

Complete Independent Movie Marketing Handbook, The: *Promote, Distribute & Sell Your Film or Video* / Mark Steven Bosko / $39.95

Creating Characters: *Let Them Whisper Their Secrets*
Marisa D'Vari / $26.95

Crime Writer's Reference Guide, The: *1001 Tips for Writing the Perfect Crime*
Martin Roth / $20.95

Cut by Cut: *Editing Your Film or Video*
Gael Chandler / $35.95

Digital Filmmaking 101, 2nd Edition: *An Essential Guide to Producing Low-Budget Movies* / Dale Newton and John Gaspard / $26.95

Directing Actors: *Creating Memorable Performances for Film and Television*
Judith Weston / $26.95

Directing Feature Films: *The Creative Collaboration Between Directors, Writers, and Actors* / Mark Travis / $26.95

Elephant Bucks: *An Insider's Guide to Writing for TV Sitcoms*
Sheldon Bull / $24.95

Eye is Quicker, The: *Film Editing; Making a Good Film Better*
Richard D. Pepperman / $27.95

Fast, Cheap & Under Control: *Lessons Learned from the Greatest Low-Budget Movies of All Time* / John Gaspard / $26.95

Fast, Cheap & Written That Way: *Top Screenwriters on Writing for Low-Budget Movies* / John Gaspard / $26.95

Film & Video Budgets, 4th Updated Edition
Deke Simon and Michael Wiese / $26.95

Film Directing: Cinematic Motion, 2nd Edition
Steven D. Katz / $27.95

Film Directing: Shot by Shot, *Visualizing from Concept to Screen*
Steven D. Katz / $27.95

Film Director's Intuition, The: *Script Analysis and Rehearsal Techniques*
Judith Weston / $26.95

Film Production Management 101: *The Ultimate Guide for Film and Television Production Management and Coordination* / Deborah S. Patz / $39.95

Filmmaking for Teens: *Pulling Off Your Shorts*
Troy Lanier and Clay Nichols / $18.95

First Time Director: *How to Make Your Breakthrough Movie*
Gil Bettman / $27.95

From Word to Image: *Storyboarding and the Filmmaking Process*
Marcie Begleiter / $26.95

Hollywood Standard, The: *The Complete and Authoritative Guide to Script Format and Style* / Christopher Riley / $18.95

Independent Film Distribution: *How to Make a Successful End Run Around the Big Guys* / Phil Hall / $26.95

Independent Film and Videomakers Guide – 2nd Edition, The: *Expanded and Updated* / Michael Wiese / $29.95

Inner Drives: *How to Write and Create Characters Using the Eight Classic Centers of Motivation* / Pamela Jaye Smith / $26.95

I'll Be in My Trailer!: *The Creative Wars Between Directors & Actors*
John Badham and Craig Modderno / $26.95

Moral Premise, The: *Harnessing Virtue & Vice for Box Office Success*
Stanley D. Williams, Ph.D. / $24.95

Myth and the Movies: *Discovering the Mythic Structure of 50 Unforgettable Films* / Stuart Voytilla / $26.95

On the Edge of a Dream: *Magic and Madness in Bali*
Michael Wiese / $16.95

Perfect Pitch, The: *How to Sell Yourself and Your Movie Idea to Hollywood*
Ken Rotcop / $16.95

Power of Film, The
Howard Suber / $27.95

Psychology for Screenwriters: *Building Conflict in your Script*
William Indick, Ph.D. / $26.95

Save the Cat!: *The Last Book on Screenwriting You'll Ever Need*
Blake Snyder / $19.95

Save the Cat! Goes to the Movies: *The Screenwriter's Guide to Every Story Ever Told* / Blake Snyder / $24.95

Screenwriting 101: *The Essential Craft of Feature Film Writing*
Neill D. Hicks / $16.95

Screenwriting for Teens: *The 100 Principles of Screenwriting Every Budding Writer Must Know* / Christina Hamlett / $18.95

Script-Selling Game, The: *A Hollywood Insider's Look at Getting Your Script Sold and Produced* / Kathie Fong Yoneda / $16.95

Selling Your Story in 60 Seconds: *The Guaranteed Way to get Your Screenplay or Novel Read* / Michael Hauge / $12.95

Setting Up Your Scenes: *The Inner Workings of Great Films*
Richard D. Pepperman / $24.95

Setting Up Your Shots: *Great Camera Moves Every Filmmaker Should Know*
Jeremy Vineyard / $19.95

Shaking the Money Tree, 2nd Edition: *The Art of Getting Grants and Donations for Film and Video Projects* / Morrie Warshawski / $26.95

Sound Design: *The Expressive Power of Music, Voice, and Sound Effects in Cinema* / David Sonnenschein / $19.95

Special Effects: *How to Create a Hollywood Film Look on a Home Studio Budget* / Michael Slone / $31.95

Stealing Fire From the Gods, 2nd Edition: *The Complete Guide to Story for Writers & Filmmakers* / James Bonnet / $26.95

Ultimate Filmmaker's Guide to Short Films, The: *Making It Big in Shorts*
Kim Adelman / $16.95

Way of Story, The: *The Craft & Soul of Writing*
Catherine Anne Jones / $22.95

Working Director, The: *How to Arrive, Thrive & Survive in the Director's Chair*
Charles Wilkinson / $22.95

Writer's Journey, – 3rd Edition, The: *Mythic Structure for Writers*
Christopher Vogler / $26.95

Writing the Action Adventure: *The Moment of Truth*
Neill D. Hicks / $14.95

Writing the Comedy Film: *Make 'Em Laugh*
Stuart Voytilla and Scott Petri / $14.95

Writing the Killer Treatment: *Selling Your Story Without a Script*
Michael Halperin / $14.95

Writing the Second Act: *Building Conflict and Tension in Your Film Script*
Michael Halperin / $19.95

Writing the Thriller Film: *The Terror Within*
Neill D. Hicks / $14.95

Writing the TV Drama Series – 2nd Edition: *How to Succeed as a Professional Writer in TV* / Pamela Douglas / $26.95

DVD & VIDEOS

Field of Fish: *VHS Video*
Directed by Steve Tanner and Michael Wiese, Written by Annamaria Murphy / $9.95

Hardware Wars: *DVD* / Written and Directed by Ernie Fosselius / $14.95

Sacred Sites of the Dalai Lamas – DVD, The : *A Pilgrimage to Oracle Lake*
A Documentary by Michael Wiese / $24.95